A BLOODY NIGHT

A BLOODY NIGHT

THE IRISH AT RORKE'S DRIFT

DAN HARVEY

MERRION
PRESS

First published in 2017 by
Merrion Press
10 George's Street
Newbridge
Co. Kildare
Ireland
www. merrionpress.ie

© 2017, Dan Harvey

9781785371295 (paper)
9781785371288 (PDF)
9781785371448 (Kindle)
9781785371455 (epub)

British Library Cataloguing in Publication Data
An entry can be found on request

Library of Congress Cataloging in Publication Data
An entry can be found on request

Cover design by wwwphoenix-graphicdesign.com

Cover front: Alphonse de Neuville, *The Defence of Rorke Drift*, 1879
(World History Archive/Alamy Stock Photo)

Dedicated to the 'Forgotten Irish' who fought, bled and died during the Anglo-Zulu War, South Africa, 1879.

CONTENTS

LIST OF ILLUSTRATIONS

PROLOGUE: FIGHT OR FLIGHT

Not long after mid-afternoon on 22 January 1879, the scene at Rorke's Drift, a ford or shallow crossing point on the Buffalo River, which at the time formed the border between the British colony of Natal and the Zulu Kingdom, was a sedate if not idyllic one, where the pace, dictated by the searing African sun, was slow and casual.

Far off, on the shimmering horizon, the glint of the sun reflected a movement that was slowly becoming more discernible. It was not identifiable other than being something incongruous to its surroundings, yet even at a distance there was something about it that demanded closer attention. As members of the garrison gazed at the horizon, the movement all of sudden took full shape as two riders emerged from the blinding light, riding fast and furiously towards them. On arrival the two badly shaken mounted infantrymen, Privates Daniel Whelan and Evans, between gasps for air and gesticulations, gave news that the British at Isandlwana camp had been ruthlessly slaughtered in great numbers by the Zulus, who were now closing fast on Rorke's Drift. In an instant the tiny garrison of the improvised supply base had to shake off any disbelief at the news, moving abruptly from a day of monotonous routine to one full of menace as they realised with dread that an unbelievable and unforeseen Zulu attack was imminent. Fear bordering on outright panic gripped them; the first and most natural inclination was to make a break for it, to put distance between themselves and danger, but that brought many other risks. Fear was inevitable, but it must not be allowed to become so overwhelming that it turned into uncontrolled terror. They had first to fight for self-control; their lives depended on it. How they reacted would determine how their story would be written.

INVASION

The discovery of diamonds in Kimberley in the 1870s offered the potential of great wealth, a fact that a number of British colonial administrators quickly grasped, but they also knew that this potential could only be fully realised by establishing British supremacy in the region. To do this, they needed to confront the independent kingdom of Zululand. Without British government approval back in London, already consumed by matters in India and particularly Afghanistan, they had somehow to find a *casus belli* to give an air of overarching legitimacy to their scheme.

The history behind this situation stretched back to the mid-seventeenth century when a shipping service station was founded by the Dutch East India Company at the Cape of Good Hope. Initially the settlement did not thrive, remaining poor for its first fifty years with fewer than 2,000 white inhabitants who were mostly Dutch but also included some Germans and French. Throughout the following century their descendants came to call themselves 'Afrikaners', speaking a variant of Dutch called 'Afrikaans', a section of whom, the 'Trekboers' (Boers), were in constant search of new grazing lands, which brought them progressively further into African territory and conflict with the native tribes. The Napoleonic Wars (1803-1815) saw Britain take permanent possession of the colony as the Cape provided a strategically important naval base on the sea-route to India and the East. The arid temperatures, however, did not appeal to potential British immigrants, so the Afrikaners remained as a majority among the white population and, with the exception of the independently minded Boers of the frontier lands, the majority were prepared to accept British writ. Continuing their search for new grazing and to escape British control, the Boer *voortrekkers* (pioneers) moved towards the north-east, establishing territories for themselves, both the Orange Free State and the Transvaal, but not of course without a series of bloody engagements with the African inhabitants. In the mid-nineteenth century Britain annexed Natal, squeezing the put-upon original African kingdoms into a space bounded between the Boers and the British. The strongest of these kingdoms was the Zulu kingdom under King Cetshwayo, leader of a proud and powerful militaristic society. In 1877 Britain annexed the Transvaal as the supposed preliminary move in an attempt to federate South Africa to mirror a system of governance that had met with some success in Canada. However, after a while it became clear to colonial administrators in British Natal that the British government in London had become reluctant to press ahead with such a move. Preoccupied with troubles enough in Afghanistan, the government's enthusiasm about engaging with a long-standing border dispute between the Transvaal and the Zulu kingdom did not match that of men like Sir Henry Frere, British High Commissioner in South Africa, Theophilus Shepstone, Chief Secretary for Native Affairs, and Lord Chelmsford, military commander in the field, who saw the continued existence of the Zulu kingdom as counter to expanding British influence, but more precisely their own interests. Time and distance from London granted then the space to implement their own scheme, which they believed they could have successfully put in place before London knew they had even begun. They were desperately looking for a provocation to undertake an expedition into neighbouring Zululand, a hostile intrusion that would have a clear and deadly intent. Chelmsford wanted to conquer the Zulu kingdom and impose British – or more correctly, 'British Colonial' – authority over it. The excuse eventually came after a Zulu prince, Mehlokazulu, had chased two of his father's errant wives across the border into Natal and bundled them back to Zululand for execution. The Zulus were given an impossible ultimatum by the colonial cabal: King Cetshwayo was to disarm, abolish his military system, pay heavy fines in the form of cattle, allow missionaries to work freely in his territories, accept a British resident to 'advise' on policy, and surrender Mehlokazulu. He was given ten days to comply. Cetshwayo was astounded and rightly understood that the British meant to destroy his kingdom, and began mustering his forces.

On 11 January 1879, Chelmsford's forces crossed the border in three separate columns with the aim of converging on the Zulu king's main residence, the Zulu capital Ulundi. Chelmsford placed himself with the centre column striking directly into the Zulu heartland. Two battalions of regular British infantry, the 1st and 2nd battalions of the 24th Regiment of Foot (2nd Warwickshires), an artillery battery of seven-pounder field guns, the Natal Native Contingent (a regiment of indigenous auxiliaries), and the Natal Native Horse left their assembly area centred around Rorke's Drift staging post and crossed their start line, the Buffalo River. The river was in full spate because the rains had finally arrived, and Chelmsford was anxious not to lose time, men or materials to possible flooding. He was also worried that the lingering mist of a drizzly morning might mask the presence of camouflaged Zulu ambush parties among the hills on the far bank. A river crossing was a fraught undertaking at any time, but even more daunting when in a raging flood and the possible hidden danger of armed opposition. The prevailing mood then was one of watchfulness and an uneasy anticipation, the atmosphere apprehensive, the moment stretched tight with tension, all senses on edge. Chelmsford, a man of great self-belief, nevertheless felt confident; all that had to happen now was to locate the Zulu king, confront him and defeat him. He was certain the Zulus were no match for his professional army with state-of-the-art weaponry. A quick and easy victory awaited, and with it the thrill of triumph, fame, and gain.

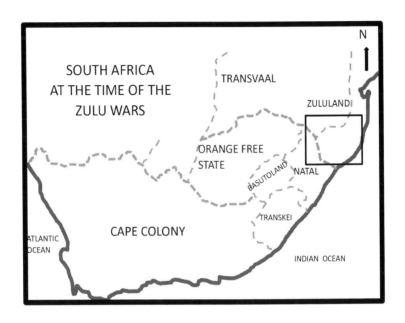

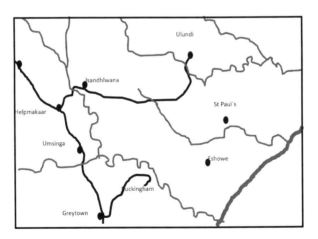

South Africa at the time of the Zulu Wars.

KWAJIMU

The logistical pipeline is a military operations lifeline. The maintenance of the integrity of the line of supply is key to success. Sustaining troops in the field allows a force to project its footprint beyond the normal range of its bases. Today's 'military speak' would refer to Rorke's Drift as an 'FOB' (a forward operating base), a secure forward military position to support tactical operations by providing back-up logistical supplies. Modern FOBs contain an airfield, logistical, communication, and transport facilities, even a hospital. These would be fortified by earthen-bank perimeter defence positions, a dry moat surround, razor-wire, watch towers, mortar pits, and weapon bays. Rorke's Drift was without any protection, completely unfortified. Located near a ford or 'drift', a place where a stream or river might be crossed by wading though it, its position on the Natal Province, 'safe', side of the Buffalo River which formed the border between British-held Natal and the Zulu Kingdom was considered protection enough. It did, however, have a 'MOB' (main operating base) ten miles back inside Natal at Helpmekaar. This supported the Rorke's Drift forward operating base with consignments of foodstuffs and military materials transported on heavily laden ox-wagons. This line of supply and communications stretched all the way rearward via Pietermaritzburg to Durban on the coast of the Indian Ocean, a seaport of disembarkation (SPOD). The responsibility for maintaining a continuity of supply was that of the Commissariat, a parallel but separate uniformed body within the military. This provisioning of food, ammunition, and other supplies was the role of individual commissaries and their teams appointed for that purpose. Rorke's Drift itself consisted of two thatched-roof buildings, the first of which was the house built around 1849 by Irishman Jim Rorke, a hunter, trader, and farmer. A once part-time soldier and the son of a full-time career soldier, he saw service in the seventh ('War of the Axe') of nine Cape Frontier Wars against the Xhosa, which ended in 1878.Seeking new adventures, he travelled north to the then new and remote frontier between Natal and Zululand. He settled on a plot of land on high ground above a favoured fording site and over the following twenty years availed of the opportunity that it and the surrounding territories offered, building his storehouse and his trading relationships on both sides of the Buffalo River. It became known as 'Jim's Land' or 'KwaJimu' to the Zulus. On his death, the trading post was sold, changing hands, perhaps at least twice. On the second occasion Otto Witt, a Swedish missionary, purchased it and converted the storehouse into a church in order to spread Christianity to the indigenous population, primarily the Zulu natives. The once trading, now missionary, post was located just over half a mile above the actual drift and nestled comfortably in a sheltered position beneath the slopes of a not insignificant hill about 330 yards to the west known as Shiyane ('The Eyebrow' or 'The Place We Left Behind').

An army's axis of advance is along a territory's main roads, in military terminology the main supply routes (MSRs). Control of these MSRs makes secure the bringing of necessary supplies to the 'front line', an unspectacular but intrinsically essential component to the achievement of victory. In South Africa in 1879 these MSRs into Zululand were few and far between and were based solely on already existing trails and tracks used by traders. Rorke's Drift gave access to one such route, and its geographical centrality made it an important point on the Buffalo River.

On his death, Jim Rorke was buried at the foot of Shiyane hill (his grave remains to this day). Many more graves would be dug there on 23 January 1879.

ADVANCE TO CONTACT

An offensive operation designed to gain contact with the enemy is an apt description of the force moving into Zulu territory across a flooded Buffalo River (Myinyathi) under the command of Lord Chelmsford, Lieutenant-General Frederick Thesiger. Chelmsford was looking for a fight, and his fear was that no fight would be offered. His three-pronged advance into Zululand was intended to flush out the Zulu *impis* (regiments) to bring about a direct, head-on confrontation with them. He wanted war.

Chelmsford's belief and expectation was that King Cetshwayo's force would avoid engaging in an open battlefield action and would favour instead indirect hit-and-run tactics. His concern was that the Zulus might attempt to slip by him and conduct a counter-strike into Natal. He wanted war with the Zulus in Zululand, and he was going to do his best to see that it happened. In his mind the chances of achieving this objective, while not guaranteed, were most likely probable. In this regard he began his coercive effort as he intended to continue, and had a small strike force hit the homesteads of the Zulu chief Sihayo KaXongo. It was his sons and followers who had supposedly violated Natal sovereignty when they retrieved the errant wives of their father and chief, providing

Chelmsford and his colonial cohorts the pretext for an invasion. This so-called infringement into Natal territory had to be seen as something that had to be punished, thus legitimizing the fraudulent *casus belli*. Chelmsford had another reason: he wanted to check the fighting capabilities of the Zulu in comparison to that of the Xhosa warriors he had defeated the previous year during the ninth Cape Frontier War, more precisely that his use of open-order tactics were the correct ones to employ. The brave but heavily outnumbered Zulu resistance he met was easily overcome, leading him to conclude that the reputation of their fighting capabilities had been greatly exaggerated, and that the future of his campaign looked favourable against such easily overcome opposition.

Camped initially on the Zulu bank of the Buffalo opposite Rorke's Drift, then near Sihayo's stronghold, Chelmsford was eager to progress his advance but the rains, especially the heavy nightly downpours, had made a muddy mire of the wagon track. It had first to be rendered useable before just a few heavily laden ox-wagons churned it up into a completely impossible quagmire. Thus his engineers went into combat with the conditions, augmented by working parties digging ditches to channel the flow of rainwater, and after nine days they were able to make the track useable. On 20 January Chelmsford with 4,000 men of No. 3 Column, complete with attendant ox-wagons laden with supplies, struck for the next stage of advance, a temporary base camp at the forward slope of a towering 500-foot high, sphinx-like rocky outcrop known as Isandlwana, so named because it resembled 'the second stomach of a ruminant cow'; it had taken Chelmsford nine days to travel ten miles. He did not intend to remain at Isandlwana for long, as he was eager to move his column in the direction of the Zulu line of advance from their capital and seat of King Cetshwayo at Ulundi. Anticipating that the Zulu forces were most likely somewhere in the range of hills to the south-east, he quickly dispatched patrols into them to keep himself situationally aware.

An experienced and competent commander, Chelmsford had an early association with Ireland. In 1882, having previously purchased a commission and a later exchange into the Grenadier Guards, he became aide-de-camp to the Lord Lieutenant of Ireland, Lord Eglington, and then to the Commander-in-chief of Ireland, Sir Edward Blakeney, from 1853 to 1854. He went on to serve in the Crimean War and the Indian Rebellion of 1857, gaining 'mentions in dispatches' in both. In India he befriended the governor of Bombay, Sir Henry Bartle Frere, and the relationship would be renewed later in South Africa. During the Expedition to Abyssinia (1868) he was awarded a CB (Companion of the Order of Bath) and appointed aide-de-camp to Queen Victoria. Subsequent appointments saw him promoted to major-general in March 1877 and to command of the forces in South Africa in February 1878, bringing the Ninth Cape Frontier War to completion five months later. He formed a low opinion of the fighting capabilities of the Xhosa warriors there and now believed the same of the Zulu.

The situational awareness required by a commander in the field is as much an art as a skill. To be aware of what is going on though reports from spy networks and scouts is one thing, to understand how this information and one's subsequent actions impact on the mission objective is another. Chelmsford's complacency and conceit proved an impediment to understanding what he was up against. When a report reached him that one of his patrols had run into a large band of Zulu warriors, and the Zulu party's reaction was to withdraw, using the fading light of dusk and the nature of the terrain to prevent the British accurately assessing their strength, Chelmsford was all too willing to believe that this behaviour confirmed how he preconceived the likely action of the main Zulu force, by being located where he felt they would be and by their unwillingness to engage with him. Interpreting this as his chance, he resolved to act and to march out and meet them. Taking a large flying column from Isandlwana, approximately half of Colonel Richard Glyn's command, mostly the 2nd Battalion of the 24th Foot and 4th Artillery, he left camp before dawn on 22 January to seek out and confront the Zulus. Before departing, Lieutenant-Colonel Henry Pulleine was placed in charge of some sixty officers and around 1,300 men, a mixture of British troops and native levies from Natal. There were some additional civilian workers also. Five companies of the First Battalion of the 24th Regiment were the lead unit *in situ*. Ordering Pulleine 'to defend the camp' (simple but significant words), Chelmsford and his force quietly left camp in the early morning darkness, moving south-east in hopeful anticipation of a confrontation with the Zulus.

On the move also at a steady pace, but evading detection, were the Zulu *impis* as they approached stealthily, almost in a choreographed fashion. They had advanced from Ulundi, having gathered for the military muster, but fortuitously the vast majority of the regiments had in fact already gathered there to partake in the annual first fruits ceremony. The timing was purely coincidental. Having correctly comprehended that the British wanted war, Cetshwayo had begun to assemble his army, and his regiments were marshalled at Ulundi to prepare for battle. This involved preparatory purification (from evil or darkness) rituals and also to engender a sense of unity, honour, and purpose: ceremonial vomiting for spiritual cleansing, rival regiments dancing as they issued boasts and challenges, medicine men and herbalists armed with cow-tails flicking protective unguents over the fighting men, and the drinking of the magical brew concocted from the masculine body parts of defeated enemies. Those who had guns – obsolete weapons from the Napoleonic era bought or taken from the Vortrekkers in the 1830s and other European traders since – held them down so that the smoke from various burning potions and medicines wafted into the barrels, thus ensuring, they believed, a straight and true aim. All this ritualistic ceremony had but one purpose: to make ready and motivate men for war; and it worked. Filled with a sense of purpose, confidence, and determination, the Zulu warriors went out to 'eat up' the invader.

Both sides were converging, but the Zulus more elusively and more situationally aware, which would give them the advantage when the inevitable clash came. They had been constantly watching Chelmsford's moves and anticipating his next. The warrior chiefs fully appreciated the importance of what today is called the 'OODA loop' by strategists – the tactical cycle of *observing*, *orienting*, *deciding*, and *acting*. They knew it was a winning strategy to get inside Chelmsford's 'OODA loop', not just by making decisions more quickly and having better situational awareness, but by even changing the situation in ways that the British could not monitor or even comprehend. It was a huge and tragic irony that Chelmsford, with his modern army and state-of-the-art weaponry against the Zulus with their primitive rituals and weaponry, believed that victory would be ensured by simply making contact with the enemy. He had lost his own situational awareness, which was the same as putting himself and his invading army 'out of the loop'. The Zulu were a more sophisticated foe than he, a career soldier and no fool, could ever imagine.

THE PEOPLE OF HEAVEN

When the Zulus fought it was fast, furious, and direct. Theirs was a martial mentality; they were warriors first, cattle herders and artisans second. They were proud and eager to engage in the fight, their courage almost suicidal and their endurance legendary. Zulu society, culture and identity were strong and strikingly successful. Some had old, often obsolete firearms but most were armed only with spears, clubs and large ox-hide shields; nonetheless, in battle they were formidable. Their strength lay in the numbers they could mobilise, and moreover those numbers were structured and well organised, backed up by standardised training and tactics. Conscription gathered diverse clan members from all over and built a homogenous kingdom with a strong sense of its own identity. Regiments were the building blocks, the backbone of a powerful army that transformed a small people into a powerful military state.

Centred on the south-eastern coast of Africa they were originally one among other tiny ethnic groups located in what today is called Zululand, lying along the steep grasslands between the Drakensberg Mountains and the Indian Ocean. A series of powerful kings shaped the Zulu destiny. Initially existing within just ten square miles, the Zulus expanded their territory steadily through progressive military success over other small rival groups until after a period known as 'The Crushing' they had forged for themselves a territory of some 12,000 square miles with an army of 40,00 from a population of about 250,000 people.

A dramatic development came with the uniting of the northern Nguni people with the Zulu kingdom, under the leadership of Shaka Kasenzangakhona, or 'Shaka Zulu'. He is credited as being the instigator of new fighting methods, organisation and weaponry, moreover instilling a more martial mentality among his warriors. He made the Zulu more belligerent, but more effectively so, with high-tempo training, tactics, and techniques. He introduced conscription, boys and men giving service to the king and not to the tribal chief. Regiments were formed by age, removing localised loyalties. The right to marry became his gift, a reward for loyalty, whole regiments sometimes taking brides all together. Once wed, the individual's primary responsibility became chiefly, but not exclusively, to the farm homestead. He was still liable to be called upon if needed. The Zulus lived in a network of small self-sustaining close family groups in scattered hamlets on hillsides and valleys. These homesteads were the core of Zulu society and were made up typically of a circular collection of huts enclosed within a fence, each hut itself a circular beehive-like shape consisting of a wooden framework thatched with grass. Contained within each was the one-roomed residence of one wife and her children. Prestige and position were determined by how many wives a man took to himself, but cattle were the real measure of wealth. The one-family homesteads surrounded the centralised cattle-kraal. The centre was regarded as a safe place for such important resources. Practical in terms of defence, the hamlets also fostered a sense of belonging and were the cornerstone of Zulu community life. A clan could consist of any number of homesteads, each with their own cattle-kraals, spread throughout a locality, more often on the eastern slopes of hills, and presided over by a local headman (*umnumzana*) with authority to adjudicate over minor disputes but also to represent them, as these headmen were in turn grouped together and presided over by a higher headman (*induna*) who acted as a judge over an extended area and collected taxes; he also heard appeals from the lower court, held a military position, and was a representative at a national level. It was a simple system, yet highly effective, and was integrated wholly into Zulu daily life.

As a young warrior Shaka Zulu customised his own broad-blade spear, adopting a shorter spear for close-quarter, hand-to-hand combat and this became the spear of choice over the longer narrow-bladed 'throwing spear' for his fighters. He also ushered in the use of larger shields and did away with sandals, making his warriors go barefoot, thus improving their mobility. This tactic of engaging at close quarters also had associated with it a method of movement, both simple and deadly, called 'the horns of the beast' (*L'mpondo Zankhoma*), the traditional Zulu method of fighting. Essentially a means of double-encirclement of the enemy, it was executed at speed and in numbers in order to achieve a swift victory. Shaka trained his warrior *impis* (regiments) to act independently in effecting this collective manoeuvre. An attacking force once unleashed in combat was difficult to control, so the manoeuvre was practised until it became second nature to his warriors. The Zulu fighters almost automatically conformed to this moving formation in the field, and the only issue to be decided on each occasion was the precise 'order of battle' (which regiment went where) within the set tactical configuration. The 'horns' were the element of encirclement, the flanking parts that set out to surround the enemy position; the 'chest of the beast' was the main body of massed warriors that drew the enemy in, engaged it, and fixed it in position; the 'loins of the beast' were the reserve, committed only when required. Once fully deployed, 'the horns of the beast' manoeuvre was brutally effective, the enemy being enveloped and then crushed.

The proficiency of the Zulu 'killing machine' involved not only martial and material arrangements but mental ones also, specifically ritualistic preparatory ceremonies involving medicine men, magic potions, and religious rites. Ceremonies were also held after a battle, when the enemy corpses were ritually disembowelled. This slitting open of the stomach and the extraction of the entrails was not a needless act of primitive barbarity but in their minds an act of spiritual self-preservation which released the spirits of the slain enemy and thus ensured they would not haunt the slayers.

The Zulu warriors of 'the People of Heaven' became a formidable force and were greatly feared. In the years following Shaka Zulu's reign, with the coming of the whites, the battles with the Boers, and civil war, their fortunes rose and fell until King Cetshwayo managed to reinvigorate the Zulu nation and its army, which once again regained its shape and power, becoming a force not to be underestimated.

British soldier from the 24th Regiment of Foot.

Illustration by Ray Fitzpatrick

THE ARMY OF EMPIRE

Firepower was the most decisive factor on the battlefield and whoever brought the most of it to bear invariably won. More precisely, it was the effect that massed, well-packed lines of infantry produced by steadily delivering a constant out-pouring of volley fire that mattered. In short, it was its 'stopping power' that was important. Fighting formation brought firepower to bear. Traditionally, during the Napoleonic Wars (1803-15), the singular soldier, with his muzzle-loaded smoothbore flintlock 'Brown Bess' musket, was virtually useless alone, but with others could be highly effective. The rate of fire, range, and accuracy determined the musket's effect. These were slow, short, and inaccurate, respectively. However, combined and continuous discharged volumes of volley fire in groups could be harnessed to give deadly effect, especially if fire was held until the enemy had closed to within fifty yards or less.

To achieve the effective use of all available muskets, or the greater part thereof, a defensive formation appropriate to the circumstances combined with steadiness in the ranks was key. Individual mastery of weapon handling was crucial and it was here the highly trained British soldier had earned a reputation for a steady, well-practised proficiency. To achieve a high rate of fire (at the time, three rounds per minute) without wavering, the soldier had to be highly trained, well drilled, and disciplined. The 'Brown Bess' or 'Indian Pattern', being a muzzle-loaded weapon, required the soldier to stand up to do so and since it was a flintlock, the mechanics of firing were somewhat involved. Suffice to say that loading, aiming, and firing was a complicated process, requiring twenty individual movements to fire each round. Reliable infantry in separate entities of a cohesive whole were trained to fire at the same moment, or to provide a continuous running volley, the entire formation delivering their murderous execution by maintaining a steadiness in the ranks and a consistency in volume. To achieve this effect in battle, well-trained infantry still needed to be well led. In the early nineteenth century officers in the British army received their commissions by purchase, while advancement was secured by payment, seniority, or patronage. A vacancy had to exist, and he who sought it had to have money to buy it. Merit or talent had little bearing on the matter. The sons of landed gentry provided their fair share of officers to the army and navy, and these 'gentlemen' were literate, could ride and shoot, and possessed a natural authoritative air and an innate sense of fairness. So the system worked. The aristocracy, however, contrary to popular belief, was by no means all-pervasive among the officer ranks, which also included the sons of professionals, 'gentlemen in trade', smaller landowners and farmers, and, of course, sons of serving or retired officers. Land, wealth, and education, all together or separately, were the all-important qualifications, and of them all the ability to read and write proved the great social divider.

Firepower was, of course, also provided by artillery. The Royal Engineers and the Royal Artillery trained their officers before giving them commissions, and only on passing their exams. A rigid adherence to seniority meant promotion was slow and would have been more so had it not expanded threefold between 1791 and 1814, and and the Royal Military Academy at Woolwich, established in 1741, was hard put to keep pace with the call for officers.

Cavalry were designated as 'heavy' and 'light', called dragoons and hussars respectively, depending on the role they were designated to undertake. Heavy cavalry was used primarily for set-piece charges, for the injection of shock and collision into the attack to give momentum and gain the initiative when closing in on infantry. The role of the light cavalry was raiding, reconnaissance, rendering advance posts to protect against surprise, and sending out of patrols. Since Waterloo the British had adopted a third cavalry designation, lancers, their eleven-foot-long lances allowing them to spear opponents and present a fearsome sight, especially terrifying to the unexperienced.

These, then, were the assets of infantry, artillery, and cavalry, the elements with which to do battle. It was the combined use of this panoply of 'moving parts' and the effects they could create at crucial times that formed the 'art of war', the purpose of which was in essence to manoeuvre the firepower of the fighting formation to where and when it would have the greatest effect. Troops had to be drilled into adopting such concentrated formations. Well-trained British troops (one third of whom were Irish) formed the backbone of the Anglo-Allied army which together with their Prussian allies defeated Napoleon at Waterloo. After Waterloo, forty years of peace had done little to prepare the British army for the experiences of the Crimean War (1854-56), in which the unified system of drill which had formed the basis of British infantry tactics during the Napoleonic Wars was again utilized. In the Crimean campaign the musket was replaced by the newly designated Enfield Pattern rifle-musket, more than half a million of which were produced over the following fourteen years. Rifle-barrelled and muzzle-loaded, its range and accuracy were a big improvement on the 'Brown Bess'. Despite this, however, a run-down and scandalously neglected army had taken to the field. The British army in Crimea, at least forty per cent of which was made up by Irishmen, consisted of one cavalry and five infantry divisions, all of which were under strength. It was led by men far too old for active service and who were inexperienced at command in war. The fossilisation in military thought, the economies that had been put in place, and the remarkably inefficient system of decentralised higher command had all contributed to the muddle and the madness that characterised the campaign. There was a serious administrative and organisational disconnect, resulting, for instance, in crucial supplies being left unloaded aboard ships, those in authority either unaware that they existed or not bothering to enquire about them. Two tried and tested units critical to battle support, the Wagon Train, responsible for carrying supplies to wherever needed, and Staff Corps, officers who analysed courses of action and different options, had both been abolished on the cessation of the Napoleonic threat.

An integral part of Victorian culture, the army of the British Empire witnessed in the wake of the Crimean War a changed, more publicly prominent perspective and a greater appreciation of the role of the ordinary soldier in war. This was unprecedented. The new focus highlighted a more sensitive depiction of the soldier's plight in the often pitiful circumstances he found himself in and caught the popular mood in a manner not seen before. The courage and endurance of the ordinary British rank and file found purchase in print, poetry, and painting. Among the dispatches from the front in Crimea, those of Irishman William Howard Russell (1820-1907) in *The Times* had a major impact on the public imagination, bearing witness as they did to the appalling conditions, including cold, hunger, and disease (mostly cholera) faced by British soldiers in the field. These and other privations, particularly during the harsh winter of 1854-55, amidst the other chaotic conditions of war, made the authorities, politicians, and the public aware of the need for change. And not only newspapers, but popular poetry such as Tennyson's conveyed the fixed determination and matter-of-fact stoicism of the soldier's previously unsung heroism. Paintings as well, most notably those by Lady Butler (Elizabeth Thompson, 1846-1933) were hugely popular, especially 'The Roll Call' (1874), a sombre picture of the Grenadier Guards mustering in the cold grey light after an engagement, which illustrated what it was like to be an infantryman bearing the physical and emotional marks of conflict.

The Royal Commission of 1858, established in the aftermath of the Crimean War, reported in 1862, but few of its recommendations were implemented due to the opposition of 'die-hard', reform-resistant senior military officers. Earlier, in January 1856, Queen Victoria herself had been quite innovative by instituting a military decoration to honour acts of valour during war. Since then, the Victoria Cross (VC) medal has been awarded to 1,355 individual recipients, more than 180 of whom were Irish. The first ever award of the medal was to Irishman Charles Lucas of *HMS Hecla*, who came from Co. Monaghan.

It was, however, the Franco-Prussian War (1870-71) and the manner of Prussian victory that shook the evident complacency from the British establishment. No longer could they continue to exist in the false comfort of fallacy, the delusionary status quo of so-called defence. The military climate in Europe had begun to change. In response to the potential Prussian threat, the British Parliament in early August 1870 approved the monies for the recruitment of 20,000 additional troops. The prior provision of the 25,000-strong army for the Crimean War had practically denuded the country of every serving soldier on the 'home front', a situation that was repeated immediately after to meet the requirement to suppress the Indian Mutiny (1857). The momentum for this enlargement had been seized upon by the Secretary of State for War, Edward Cardwell, who, with the support of William Gladstone, the Liberal Prime Minister, introduced measures to update the army, bringing real change to bear by firstly centralizing the power of the War

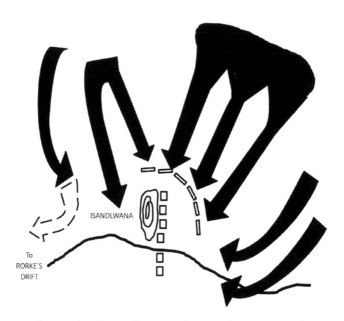

The Battle of Isandlwana, showing the advance of the Zulus.

Office, then abolishing the system of purchasing officers' commissions, and secondly by creating a strategic reserve at home. The Cardwell reforms (1870-81) initially addressed the abolition of flogging, at first at home and later on active service abroad. It was considered imperative to discharge men of bad character and attract instead good quality recruits; consequently, the seven-year short service option was introduced, which was later extended to ten years and then to twelve. The withdrawal from overseas territories saw 26,000 troops come back from far-flung, self-governing colonies where locally raised forces began to manage their own defence. A functioning reserve was raised at home, and in a hugely significant move, Cardwell divided Great Britain and Ireland into sixty-six regimental districts, thus 'teritorializing' the infantry where each regiment became associated with a particular county. There were to be two battalions per regiment, with one battalion serving overseas and the other garrisoned at home for training. Each regiment had a training depot and associated recruiting areas. Militia units would make up a third battalion. The reforms also extended to improving the Spartan living conditions of the soldier. The frugal barrack-room furniture had been basic, with rudimentary beds, benches, and tables. Sheets were now changed monthly, and the straw in the mattresses was replaced every three months. A four-and-a-half penny deduction for rations in the one shilling per day pay was abolished in 1873. The infantry was re-equipped with the first proper breech-loading rifle, the Martini-Henry, the best service rifle of its day. The process of loading, aiming, firing, reloading was speeded up, and there was now the possibility of firing eight rounds a minute. A rapid-fire, accurate weapon, it fired a large calibre bullet over a significant distance, packing a heavy punch. Its big bullet inflicted severe wounds and had noteworthy stopping power. A single-shot, breech-loading, lever-actuated service rife, it was activated by pulling down the lever behind the trigger guard, which engaged the mechanism, whereby the now uncovered breech ejected the spent cartridge case, the firer reloading by taking a bullet from his pouch and pressing it into the rifle's chamber. Its introduction significantly increased the firepower capacity of the British Infantry. It was a hugely valuable addition to the infantryman then engaged it what became termed Victoria's 'Little Wars', in effect the suppression of uprisings occurring inconveniently in any of the British Empire's colonies which at the time stretched across a quarter of the globe. It was an army of 150,000 men in 140 infantry battalions, in addition to which were artillery and cavalry regiments, all with technologically advanced firepower. In 1878, 40,000 Irishmen or twenty-two per cent of the British army were Irish. Of the British army element in South Africa in 1879, there was the inevitable strong Irish element in evidence, attracted by the lure of travel and adventure, the quest for soldiering, or more likely for economic reasons, the escape from poverty. For one, some, or all of these reasons the Irish 'were there'.

'DAY OF THE DEAD MOON':
THE BATTLE OF ISANDLWANA

The two lead scouts of the small scouting party from Isandlwana threw unbelieving glances at each other, then turned their heads again in the direction of the valley to confirm what they had just seen. They were in no doubt as to what they were witnessing, but they could not comprehend how it was possible. One minute there had been a valley typically nestled among rolling hills of grasslands with little visible activity. The next minute, there was a valley with thousands of Zulus sitting silently on the valley floor. In today's parlance, they had accidentally 'bumped' into the entire Zulu main force that Chelmsford was elsewhere actively seeking, desperate to engage with and destroy it. But while he searched among the hills in the south-east, here they were among those in the north-east, 20,000 of them sitting quietly on the Ngwebeni valley floor only five miles from Isandlwana camp, not at all where they were expected to be and poised to do what they were not expected to do, offer the battle Chelmsford so recklessly sought.

The Zulus had in fact not expected that they would be discovered, their presence having been stumbled on by chance. Their successful stealthy approach, arriving so close to the British camp, was a major achievement of manoeuvrability. Their intent was to exploit the initiative to its fullest the following day, for today was 'the day of the dead moon', a day prior to a moonless night and so, according to their beliefs, deemed unsuitable for combat. Once discovered, however, the Zulus' immediate reaction was like the release of a coiled spring, with those nearest the startled scouts instantly leaping up to run towards them, the entire Zulu army following behind. The initial Zulu disorder developed quickly through discipline and long practice into their favoured attacking formation, the shape of the encircling 'loin, chest, and horns of the beast', although it was not the exact order of battle they had planned to adopt.

As the pulsating waves of warriors broke the crest of the hill and began to descend towards Isandlwana, the two shocked scouts joined the remainder of the scouting party whose commander wisely dispatched a rider rearward to warn Lieutenant-Colonel Pulleine, camp commander, of the Zulus' approach. In the interim, Pulleine had been joined by Irishman Colonel Anthony Dunford, commander of No. 2 Column whom Chelmsford had ordered forward, and approximately 250 men of the Natal Native Horse. When news of the Zulu activity had reached camp it was not viewed as particularly alarming, nonetheless the 1st Battalion of the 24th Regiment of Foot were prudently 'stood to', but with no particular sense of urgency as, to be fair to Pulleine, he had no real idea of the Zulu numbers or their exact intent, besides which he had the battalion of a professional, modern army under his command equipped with the Martini-Henry rifle. Dunford with his mounted party rode out to investigate and the men of the 1st/24th Foot steadied themselves for a possible defence of the camp while at the same time not at all ready or prepared for what was about to unfold.

The Zulu offensive, executed with audacity and speed, meant that from the moment of its inception, triggered by the scouts' chance discovery, the fate of the British at Isandlwana was sealed. The Zulu surge had started, steadily traversing the undulating open terrain covered with tall grasses and dotted with rocky outcrops and crisscrossed with gullies and dried-out river beds called *dongas*. Each successive forward stride by the massed warriors was inexorably leading to the inevitable destruction of a British force completely caught off balance, and it would not be long in arriving.

'March slowly, attack at, dawn, and eat up the red soldiers,' was King Cetshwayo's command to Ntshingwayo and Mavumengwana, the two chiefs he had placed in charge some five days beforehand as he sent them out from Ulundi. This 24,000-strong force crossed the White Umfolozi river on the following day, when 4,000 warriors detached themselves to strike against the British No. 1 Column under Charles Pearson at Eshowe. The main body moved tactically in easy stages over fifty miles in five days, first via the Babanango then the Siphezi Mopenountains and next to the Isiphezi Ikhanda, and finally onto its concealed position in the Ngwebeni valley, poised to attack the British at first light on 23 January. Preceded by a screening force of a few hundred to prevent the main force from being sighted, the main body moved in two separate columns a few miles apart while still keeping within sight of each other to prevent against a surprise attack, and skilfully using the undulating terrain to mask their movement and evade Chelmsford's scouts until they reached their 'hide' in the Ngwebeni valley. Their untimely discovery here upset the timing of their attack but not the plan, which was still viable and was now being executed.

The arrangement of natural features within the area of a battlefield has great relevance because, when examined closely, it can explain important aspects, maybe even the essence of the conflict that took place there. Military experts analyse terrain in relation to the advantages and disadvantages it may bestow in either defence or attack, with possible avenues of approach, obstacles, cover and concealment, and other key aspects all considered. At Isandlwana, several hundred yards from the camp, was a slight rise beyond which the ground dipped into a hollow across which *dongas* ran, the ground further out again rising to an escarpment, a steep slope at the edge of a plateau. This first rise, although quite far out from the camp, presented a tactical advantage for any troops placed on it to fire down into the hollow, turning it into a 'killing ground'. It was along here that Pulleine deployed his defence in an open order, elongated firing line at right angle to the camp on its left side. Distant gunfire could be heard out far, the scouting party and Dunford's men now beginning to engage with the Zulus whose ever-advancing massed force was still invisible to the camp's defenders. Colonel Dunford, born in Manorhamilton, Co. Leitrim, to a family associated with the Royal Engineers since 1759, was educated in Ireland and Germany before going to the Royal Military Academy at Woolwich. Commissioned into the Royal Engineers, he was to miss active service in Crimea because of a bout of fever contracted in Ceylon. Postings to England and Gibraltar saw him missing out on further active service in India, China, New Zealand, and the North-West Frontier. Once a vacancy for a Royal Engineers officer was offered in the Cape Colony, Dunford grabbed it, arriving in 1872. Africa suited him, and he it. He had an empathy towards the Xhosa and a sympathy for them in relation to the Boer encroachment on their lands. In mid-1873 he was posted to Natal and in due course was appointed by Chelmsford to raise a native auxiliary force, the Natal Native Contingent (NNC). In 1878 he was invited to join Chelmsford's staff and was offered command of the No. 2 Column. It was his plans for 'floating bridges', the pontoons, that saw the British cross over the Buffalo River, and he was also the one to produce maps from which the staff were to work. He did not favour the military intervention into Zululand, but as a soldier it was not an adventure he was likely to pass on. He was certainly energised by the excitement of the escapade he was now entangled in, doing his utmost to ensure that he did not become ensnared by the Zulu 'left horn' advancing down the escarpment.

As this 'fighting retreat' continued, Pulleine placed the companies of the 1st/24th and one of the 2nd/24th into a firing line formation with a large frontage. The soldiers were not shoulder to shoulder, rather there was an interval of two to three yards between each. He placed a reliance on the stopping power of the Martini-Henry rifle to swing the battle in his favour. Theoretically his conjecture was correct, as the rifle packed a significant 'punch', and as far as he was concerned, he was going to meet his attackers head-on. The 24th was an experienced regiment, its men having seen action before. This combination of factors were, he believed, sufficient to see off whatever threat from local assailants was gathering unseen beyond the skyline. Only it was not a partial force from the particular area they were up against but, more forebodingly, the substantive army of the entire Zulu nation. This absence of alarm fundamentally undermined his estimation of the situation, and the open-order firing line was placed well out in front (archaeological investigations conducted in 2000 found it to be further out that initially thought). Eventually, Dunford's men appeared into the defenders' line of sight, the 'left horn' of the Zulu attack not far behind. Next, the 'chest' crested the hill, descended from the heights and came into the 'killing ground' of the hollow and so within the line of fire of the defenders who duly poured lead into them. The 'thump' of the fired round was loud, the recoil heavy, the effect deadly. The Zulus, however, were both determined and disciplined. More, they were prepared psychologically and pharmacologically, and consumed with blood lust. They were a unified mass with a common sense of purpose, to smash the British camp. It was all about the contest between the British rate of fire and the Zulu rate of advance. The intensity of fire won initially against the driving force of movement, and with the attack stalled, the Zulus took cover in the broken ground of the gullies and the *dongas*. The Zulu chief Ntshingwayo sent down an *izinduna* ('war doctor') who, standing erect among the crouching Zulus, stirred them into action, whereupon they rose up, roared their battle-cry, and rushed forward up the slope to meet the British line. In the meantime, more Zulus were arriving from the rear and, finding the advance stalled and their way forward blocked, began to pile up and spill out sideways, forcing the 'left horn' to manoeuvre further left, thus threatening the rear of the British right flank. If the British rate of fire had temporarily won out over the Zulu rate of advance, the Zulu weight of numbers was now winning out against the British weight of fire. Even the effects of the two British seven-pounder artillery pieces did not deter for long the Zulu advance. Having observed the 'gunners' drill, they dropped into the long grass and, having waited for the projectiles to land, sprung up and counter-attacked shouting, 'Lightning, lightning of heaven. See its glittering flash', while others shouted, 'It is only wind'. An ordered 'fire and retreat' formation was maintained for a while until the Zulu impetus impacted against the defensive line which collapsed completely.

The elongated, too thin, too far forward, and dangerously overstretched firing line, always potentially porous, was penetrated. Once through the gaps, the Zulus picked up their pace, their advance now becoming an assault conducted in great numbers from the flanks and the front. It was overpowering, the defence buried beneath a huge mass. The resulting immense carnage was inevitable. Killing at close quarters began, the fighting primeval, savage, and barbaric. But the survival instinct is strong, and the defenders were not going to sell their lives cheaply. Broken up into groups, the integrity of the whole defence shattered, the defenders fell back under pressure and, attempting to bring order to disorder, formed squares at various scattered rallying points. Desperate last stands were made by groups and individuals, fighting hopelessly for their lives, each knowing they were facing a bloody and brutal annihilation. In some places the greater part of companies or remnants of a few companies formed together to offer a collective defence; as long as they could maintain a heavy fire they were able to keep their Zulu attackers at bay. This state could only hold, however, as long as their ammunition lasted, and then it was no-holds-barred, hand-to-hand primitiveness. Spears were flung, bayonets thrust, skulls smashed, bodies slashed, limbs severed,; there was pain, shock, and fear; there were heroes and cowards, leaders and led, defenders and attackers dead and dying. The Zulus showed no mercy, and there was little hope of escape. But against all the odds some did, only to find to their horror that the route to freedom was cut off. Of those who did make a successful getaway, it was because they were mounted on a horse, and only before the 'right horn' of the Zulu attack completed the encirclement. One of those who made a bold bid for freedom was Lieutenant Nevill Coghill, born in Drumcondra, Dublin, now serving with the 1st/24th. In this fraught pursuit of safety he found himself accompanied by Lieutenant Teignmouth Melvill, also mounted, an adjutant of the 1st/24th who had taken possession of the battalion's Queen's Colour (each infantry regiment had two Colours, Regimental and Queen's) and was attempting to remove it from the field to safety so that it would not fall into Zulu hands, an event that would have been perceived as a disgrace as the Colour was the physical embodiment of regimental pride and loyalty to Queen and country. Together they were able to escape from the battlefield, unlike others who were not on horseback and were cut down by the Zulus, and rode a precarious route of three miles or so to reach the Buffalo River downstream of Rorke's Drift. Their perils were not at an end, however, as the river was in flood and fast flowing. Both entered on horseback and while Coghill reached the safety of the far river bank on the Natal side, Melvill fell victim to the raging torrent, became unhorsed, and was swept away. He managed, however, to hold on tightly to a boulder along the river's course but he was unable to keep a grip of the Colour, which disappeared in the current. Coghill immediately came to his aid and despite the hostile presence of Zulus firing at them from the river bank he managed, with the aid of a Native Contingent officer, Lieutenant Higginson, to save Melvill. All three, exhausted, then encountered new hostilities from local warriors encouraged by the Zulus. Higginson went to locate stray horses, and Coghill and Melvill were overcome in an uneven fight. The Colour was to be eventually found and restored. Coghill and Melvill were posthumously awarded the Victoria Cross.

Back at Isandlwana, a Zulu warrior described a sudden eerie darkness, an eclipse of the sun: 'The sun turned black in the middle of the battle, we could still see it over us, or we should have thought we were fighting till evening. Then we got into the camp and there was a great deal of smoke and firing and afterwards the sun came out again.' The annihilation continued unabated, the defenders fighting to the death. Some 1,300 of 1,600 men were killed. Most of the survivors were native auxiliaries, and fewer than sixty British troops, all mounted, managed to escape the butchery. It has been estimated that there were 1,000 Zulu dead and approximately the same number of wounded. It had been a great Zulu victory, an outcome that shook Victorian Britain to the core; though technologically inferior, they had 'eaten up the red soldiers'.

In opting for dispersion rather than concentration, open order rather than closed, and forming a firing line far out rather than one large square closer to the camp, the British had greatly reduced their chances of survival. A great deal of investigation and soul-searching has been conducted into the defeat, blame apportioned, scapegoats sought, and myths created. However, getting the measure of the enormous moving mass of 20,000 Zulus was always unlikely for the surprised British once

At the final sequence at the Battle of Isandlwana.

the momentum of their advance had gathered impetus. Once begun, it was unstoppable. The British were unable to prevent envelopment. The odds and circumstances were overwhelming, and any defence untenable. An appreciation of the scope of the threat was beyond them until it was all too late. And for this, Chelmsford's conceit alone was responsible. His arrogance had prevented him from comprehending the real threat; he regarded the Zulus with contempt, and it was the soldiers on the field at Isandlwana who were to pay the price with their lives.

There were numerous Irish among them, men named Bennett, Collins, Connolly, Donohue, Kelly, Mahony, Murphy, Burke, Fitzgerald, Harrington, Holland, Egan, Walsh, and more. The 24th Foot at Isandlwana had many Irish with them, including 38-year-old Private William Griffiths VC from Co. Roscommon. He had been awarded the Victoria Cross for the gallant manner in which, some twelve years previously, on 7 May 1867, during the Andaman Islands Expedition. He and four others had risked their lives in manning a boat and proceeding through a dangerous surf to rescue some of their comrades, who had landed, and were supposed to have been murdered by the cannibalistic native islanders. Surviving intrepidly on that occasion, he was now among the slaughtered victims of an unnecessary war. It is the politician that commits a nation to conflict, it is the soldier that has to sort out the mess.

Saving the Colours *by Alphonse de Neuville.*

ESTIMATE OF THE SITUATION

The impact of the news of the terrible slaughter of comrades at Isandlwana was shocking and filled those at Rorke's Drift with a revulsion that was quickly followed by fear and foreboding with the realisation that a large force of highly belligerent Zulus was on its way to the post and not far off. It was a case of having to take in news that was almost incomprehensible and face up to a new stark reality all at once. Such a crisis was likely to cause a range of competing emotions and, if not mental paralysis, a titanic struggle to achieve presence of mind. It was one thing to be shocked and then to have to face uncertainty, but it was another matter altogether to be suddenly propelled into a situation of extreme danger and almost certain death.

One amongst the defenders quickly took matters into his own hands, someone with the confidence and ability to control fear when facing danger and who could apply a logic that was reasonable and coherent. An expression used in Ireland, that 'he's been here before', suggests someone who has the benefit of wisdom well beyond their years, a compliment to someone's worldly experience, knowledge, and insight.

In a sense this was true of Irishman Acting Assistant Commissary James Langley Dalton. Born in 1833, he enlisted in the 85th Foot in November 1849 aged 17. He transferred to the Commissariat Corps in 1862 as a corporal and was promoted to sergeant the following year, becoming a master sergeant four years later. He served in Canada on the Red River Expedition in 1870, retiring the following year with a long service and good conduct medal after twenty-two years service. In 1877 he was in South Africa as a private individual and when volunteers were looked for he offered his services and was appointed acting assistant commissary. His role was to involve him in logistical support for British sweeps through Xhosa territory during the later stages of the Ninth Cape Frontier War in 1878. The provisioning of food, ammunition, and other supplies was the responsibility of the Commissariat and Transport Department, which became the Royal Army Service Corps in 1888. This vital support significantly assisted successful tactical deployment, extending the reach of the British columns into Xhosa territory. One logistics supply post, which Dalton was in charge of, was that at Ibeka, which became noted for its efficiency, a fact that did not escape the attention of the Xhosa who decided to move against it. They advanced first to isolate it before making ready to launch a direct attack. The occupants reacted by fortifying the depot and then took cover behind hastily prepared positions, bracing themselves for the impending assault which, to their surprise and immense relief, did not materialise. The Xhosa, deterred by the defensive measures and the defiance displayed by the depot's garrison, were discouraged and contented themselves with driving off the unattended oxen. This experience with the Xhosa at Ibeka was to prove a valuable lesson for James Dalton who in January 1879 was appointed to set up the depot at Rorke's Drift along with fellow Irishmen Walter Dunne and Louis Byrne, both in the Commissariat, and also Corporal Francis Atwood.

When the startling news was received that those at Isandlwana had been ruthlessly slaughtered in great numbers and the Zulus were on their way to attack Rorke's Drift, the commander of B Company, Lieutenant Gonville Bromhead, held a quick meeting with Dunne, Reynolds, and Dalton held to decide the best course of action: whether to attempt an immediate retreat to Helpmekaar ten miles to the rear or to make a stand where they stood. It was Dalton's cogent logic and persuasive manner that convinced the others that a small column travelling in open country and burdened with carts carrying hospital patients would be easily overtaken and overcome by a numerically superior Zulu force, and it was soon agreed that the only acceptable, although counter-intuitive, course of action was to remain and fight. According to Dunne,

> *Dalton, as brave a soldier as ever lived, had joined us, and hearing the terrible news said, 'Now we must make a defence!' It was his suggestion which decided us to form a breastworks of bags of grain, boxes of biscuits, and everything that could help stop a bullet or keep out a man.*

Courage, logic, and experience combined, Dalton applied his understanding from previous exposure to a similar encounter and unhesitatingly put into action what he had learned; after all, he had 'been here before'.

'NO POWER COULD STAND AGAINST...'

Although Lieutenant Nevill Coghill was born in Drumcondra, Co. Dublin, in 1852, his family had strong connections with Castletownshend in Co. Cork, a charmingly curious coastal locality cultivated over the centuries by a vibrant, self-organised community of Ascendancy families who lived a serene existence in close vicinity to each other in the safe and secluded moorage of Castlehaven Bay. Half-way down Castletownshend's steep-hilled main street and dividing it in two stand two splendid sycamore trees. At the foot of this hill on a slight rise is the Protestant church of Saint Barrahane in whose south wall are three Harry Clarke windows that set the altar alight with bright beams of blue and violet light which also fall on the many marble memorials to military men, among them Lieutenant Coghill. Both the British army and navy were well served by Castlehaven's manhood, both Ascendancy and non-Ascendancy, one of whom, among many others over the years, was Private Michael Minehan who on 22 January 1879, like Nevill Coghill, was serving in the Zululand Natal border area of South Africa – he as a member of B Company, 2nd Battalion, 24th Regiment of Foot at Rorke's Drift. The mission station, now converted into an improvised supply depot, was garrisoned by B Company of the 2/24th (re-designated as the South Wales Borderers in 1881) and around 300 men of the Natal

Native Contingent under the command of Major Henry Spalding of the 104th Foot. The commander of B Company was Lieutenant Gonville Bromhead. Lieutenant John Chard, Royal Engineers, was also present at the post, carrying out necessary maintenance repairs to the parts of the Drift proper. Private Michael Minehan, along with other members of B Company, were feeling somewhat deflated and disappointed at being left out of the big push into Zulu territory. As a fellow Corkonian, Assistant Commissary Officer Walter Adolphus Dunne, in charge of the stores at Rorke's Drift, put it,

> *Our post at Rorke's Drift seemed silent and lonely after they [Lord Chelmsford's Headquarters Group and Colonel Richard Glyn's No. 3 Column] had left; but we expected to join them soon and to hear of some fierce but successful fight with the enemy.*

This feeling of abandonment was to be further compounded when Colonel Anthony Dunford's No. 2 Column arrived and went forward, on Chelmsford's order, to attach itself to No. 3 Column to reinforce the camp at Isandlwana, while he with half the camp's compliment went in search of the main Zulu *impis* in the hills to the south-east. B Company were disappointed not to be crossing the Buffalo River into adventure and action with them, instead remaining on the Natal side and guarding the Rorke's Drift improvised supply depot and field hospital. Despite, however, their feeling of useless idleness and not being able to live up to their soldierly expectations, they anticipated being relieved by the already well overdue arrival of another company of the 24th, which was expected to make an appearance at any time from Helpmakaar, ten miles to their rear. Lieutenant Chard, who had been at the Isandlwana camp that morning, returned to Rorke's Drift just before noon and informed Major Spalding of Zulu movements. Spalding decided to go to

Helpmekaar to see what was delaying the company. Before departing he consulted a copy of the Army List and seeing that Chard was the senior of the two lieutenants present, informed him that he was in command. In the interim there was precious little for the garrison to do except wait until a scheduled convoy of empty wagons arrived from the column at Isandlwana to collect their re-supply stores.

Of course, the garrison at Rorke's Drift when watching their colleagues crossing the Buffalo River never realised that many of them were going to their doom. Nor could they have guessed that they themselves would shortly face their own stiff challenges and difficulties, an unimaginable testing predicament at that.

Invigorated by victory and eager for action, thousands of Zulu warriors were heading for Rorke's Drift. At the head of four Zulu regiments – the iNdluyengive ibutho, uThulwana, iNdlondho, and uDhoko – was a leader hungry for recognition, King Cetshwayo's half-brother Prince Dabulamanzi kaMpande. These were the reserve, the force kept back for emergencies, 'the loins of the beast', and had not become engaged, having swept right with the 'right horn of the beast', and so had little or no part in the great Zulu victory at Isandlwana only hours before. They were now seeking to 'wash their spears' in the blood of the tiny garrison at Rorke's Drift. These were the veterans, the older and more senior members of the Zulu army. Recognition and validation of worthy participation were important to them. But as yet they had not had that degree of involvement and they were desperately seeking to salvage some respect and pride. Prince kaMpande had impulsively ignored Cetshwayo's prior direction, not to cross the Buffalo River because as far as he was concerned 'KwaJimu' was where reputation would be rescued and status salvaged.

When the also 'left out of battle' garrison of Rorke's Drift heard gunfire around midday from the east in the Isandlwana direction they were more curious than concerned; it was as much as they had expected, having anticipated skirmishing of sorts. In fact, much of the noise of the full encounter at Isandlwana had been shielded by the intervening hills. Nonetheless, inquisitiveness got the better of some, and a group of four, armed with a telescope, went up onto the nearby Shiyane hill to investigate. Among this group was Surgeon James Henry Reynolds who was born on 3 February 1844 in Kingstown (Dun Laoghaire), Co. Dublin. His father was Laurence P. Reynolds of Dalystown House, Co. Longford. James was educated at Castleknowck College (1855-60) before entering Trinity College, Dublin, to study medicine. He received his BA (1864) and MCh (1867), joining the Army Medical Department as an assistant-surgeon on 31 March 1868. Appointed as medical officer to the 36th (the Herefordshire) Regiment of foot on 24 March 1869, he accompanied the regiment to India. During his time in India there was an outbreak of cholera and his calm attention to duty was noted. He received the thanks of the Commander-in-Chief, Lord Sandhurst, and was promoted to full surgeon in 1873. A posting to South Africa followed where he took part in the Cape Frontier War of 1877-8 and was present at the battle of Impetu. At the outbreak of the Zulu war in 1879 he was appointed medical officer to the No. 3 Central Column under Colonel Richard Glyn. When the column crossed over the Buffalo River into Zululand on 11 January 1879 he remained at Rorke's Drift, in charge of the hospital there. As the column departed he said farewell to two particular friends, Surgeon-Major Peter Shepard and Lieutenant Edgar Anstey of the 24th Foot. Both were to be killed at Isandlwana. Anstey left his dog in Reynolds' care. On the morning of 22 January Reynolds had carried out his rounds in the makeshift hospital as usual before heading up Shiyane hill to investigate the source of the gunfire. Formerly Jim Rorke's home and now the property of the Otto Witts

Swedish missionaries, the thatched-roof building was not altogether ideal for its new use as the floorplan made it difficult to circulate within. Its interior layout had no central access, and many rooms were tiny and could only be accessed through doors on the outside. A shortage of beds was overcome by raising wooden planks off the floor with bricks, and straw was used for bedding. There were thirty-six patients in the hospital suffering from dysentery, diarrhoea, and fever as well as minor ailments and injuries; only two had actual 'war wounds' – sustained by Corporals Mayer and Schiess of the Natal Native Contingent in the earlier attack on the homestead of Zulu Chief Sihayo – and unusually, the hospital also held a Zulu warrior wounded in that action.

From the vantage point of Shiyane hill, the party of four, which included Surgeon Reynolds, Chaplain George Smith, Otto Witt, and Private Wall, could see the rearward slopes of Isandlwana. Reynolds describes what unfolded,

> *At 1.30 a large body of natives marched over the top of Isandlwana in our direction, their purpose evidently being to examine ravines and ruined kraals for hiding fugitives (those escaping from Isandlwana). These men we took to be our native contingent. Soon afterwards appeared four horsemen on the Natal side of the river, galloping in the direction of our post; one of them was a regular soldier and, feeling they might be messengers for additional medical assistance, I hurried down the hill as they rode up. They looked awfully scared, and I was at once startled to find one of them was riding Surgeon-Major Shepard's pony. They shouted frantically, 'The camp at Isandlwana had been taken by the enemy and all our men in it massacred', that no power could stand against the enormous number of Zulus, and the only chance for us all was by immediate flight.*

Both groups 'left out of battle' were eager to engage, but both in turn would regret what they had wished for.

'NOW WE MUST MAKE A DEFENCE'

The situation was summed up succinctly by Surgeon Reynolds.

> *Lieutenant Bromhead, Acting-Commissary Dalton and myself forthwith consulted together, Lieutenant Chard not having as yet joined us from the pontoon, and we quickly decided that with barricades well placed around our present position a stand could best be made where we were. Just at this period Mr. Dalton's energies were invaluable. Without the smallest delay, he called upon his men to carry mealie sacks here and there for defences. Lieutenant Chard (R.E.) arrived as this work was in progress and gave many useful orders as regards the line of defence. He approved also of the hospital being taken in, and between the hospital orderlies, convalescent patients (eight or ten) and myself, we loop-holed [made firing holes] in the building and made a continuation of the commissariat defences around it. The hospital, however, occupied a wretched position, having a garden and shrubbery close by, which afterwards proved valuable to the enemy; but, comparing our prospects with that of the Isandlwana affair, we felt that the mealie barriers might afford us a moderately fair chance.*

Chard had remained at the Drift for a while supervising the securing of the parts being moored in midstream, the filling of the water cart and the loading of tools into a wagon, and for that to be brought the half mile back to the supply post. He described what he saw when he returned,

> Lieutenant Bromhead was already most actively engaged in loop-holing and barricading the stone building and hospital, and also in connecting the defence of the two buildings by walls constructed with mealie bags and wagons. I held a hurried consultation with him and Mr. Dalton of the Commissariat – who was actively superintending the work of the defence and whom I cannot sufficiently thank for his most valuable services, and I entirely approved of all his arrangements.

Dalton, having initiated the defence of Rorke's Drift, set about planning its fortification. Writing in the *Army Service Corps Journal* in 1891, Dunne was to record: 'Dalton's suggestion of fortifying the post by piling up mealie bags to form barricades, linking the store and hospital, was quickly agreed upon,' and, while Bromhead fell in the men, Dunne and Dalton traced out the lines of the ramparts on the ground.

According to Surgeon Reynolds,

> . . . without the smallest delay, which would have been so fatal for us... [Dalton] called upon the men to carry the mealie sacks here and there for defence and it was charming to find in a short time how comparatively protected we had made ourselves.

Assistant Commissary Dunne was also to explain,

> It was well for us that we had help of the 300 natives [of Captain George Stevenson's Natal Native Contingent] at this juncture, otherwise the works would not have been accomplished in time.

It is not at all clear if the number of Natal Native Contingents was in fact 300; most reliable references suggest it was more probably nearer to 100. There are some discrepancies also in relation to the precise number of 'regular' troop defenders, the lead unit, of course, being B Company 2nd/24th who together with the 'walking wounded' in the hospital, the commissariat, medical personnel, and other attachments gave a total figure of less than 140.

The next hour or so was a period which saw all hands haul out of the storehouse the 200lb bags of mealie grain and 100lb biscuit boxes and use them to fortify the post. They all understood that although the situation was indeed desperate, behind barricades there was at least a chance. While this work continued, the sensible precaution of posting sentries as lookouts and a separate party as security had been undertaken. The judicious opening of several boxes of ammunition placed at a number of points saw that most of the 20,000 rounds or so available to them were to hand, not having to be looked for later. The fortified post became a strong-point with a 360 degree perimeter, its defence having to be an all round one, and in some areas far from ideal because Jim Rorke, when he selected the site for his homestead in 1849, had not placed security as a priority, nor had done much over the years to improve it. All told, when paced out, the perimeter ran to a total length of 300 yards or so, quite small to look at, rather large to defend, and not without its vulnerable areas, due of course to the 'lie of the land'. Mid-way or so along the north perimeter wall of mealie-bags, the advantageous, slightly raised flat rock ledge on which the homestead was perched smoothened out to a more gentle incline to allow the access of wagons to the storehouse. This too was the case in front of the hospital building, the exposure made more acute by the nearness of shrubbery and a close-by garden. Ordinarily, time permitting, anything impeding line of sight and line of fire would be cleared. Any obstructions to the fall of shot, or that allowed an enemy a covered avenue of approach, would be cut down.

This clearing of fields of fire would create an open space and so become an obstacle to an advance as there would be nowhere for advancing troops to seek shelter from fire. The lack of time, however, prevented the defenders from attending to this necessary and important aspect of preparing a defensive position.

The hectic preparing of defences continued for an hour or so: the building of the barricade with mealie-bags, biscuit boxes, meat boxes, and two ox-wagons incorporated into the south wall, the dropping of the tents where B Company were accommodated, the loop-holing of the storehouse and the hospital, the mobilising of the 'walking wounded', with no time to move the bed-ridden patients, the allocating of a half dozen members of B Company with orders to reinforce the building, and the distribution of reserve ammunition. The fortifying of the post lit a small glimmer of hope in the hearts of the defenders, giving some expectation of a deeply desired security and some assurance of salvation, dearly sought after and clung to in an unpromising situation. It was cause for some degree of optimism in the midst of awful circumstances. Imagine then their elation with the surprise arrival of Lieutenant Alfred Henderson, commander of the Edendale troop previously under Colonel Anthony Dunford's Natal Native Horse Command, with about 100 mounted men, survivors of Isandlwana – a valuable addition to the garrison, enhancing their chances and adding to their confidence.

At the centre of all these preparations, with the responsibility of command suddenly thrust upon him, was 31-year-old Lieutenant John Chard of the Royal Engineers. For an army in transition, it was no longer unthinkable, but was still certainly unusual, for an engineer officer to command infantry. Affable, relaxed, he had eleven years service, three of those in Bermuda and a year in Malta, and had only recently arrived in South Africa. Subordinate to Chard was Lieutenant Gonville 'Gunny' Bromhead (33), Officer Commanding B Company, 2nd Battalion,

24th (2nd Warwickshire) Foot, which formed the garrison of the post. Bromhead was two years older than Chard and had a year and a half more service. Bromhead as a regular infantry officer had to serve over four years as a second lieutenant before becoming a lieutenant while Chard had been commissioned as a full lieutenant direct on qualification from Warwick. Bromhead was one of four sons of Major Edmund de Gonville Bromhead who had fought at Waterloo. The Bromheads were a titled Lincolnshire family with a proud military lineage: his great-grandfather, Boardman Bromhead, was with General Wolfe at Quebec, his grandfather, a lieutenant-general had fought in America's Revolutionary Wars, and both his father and uncle had fought against Napoleon. A third son, not likely to inherit the family baronetcy, his father in the twilight years of purchasing of commissions bought for him an ensign's vacancy in the 24th, whereupon he was appointed on 20 April 1867, being promoted four years later. He had seen service in India and all told had over eleven years of service before finding himself at Rorke's Drift.

A closer look at Lieutenant Gonville 'Gunny' Bromhead reveals he was born on 29 August 1845 in Versailles, France. Gonville's father, Edmund Bromhead, was half-Irish, his mother, Judith Wood from Co. Sligo, fully Irish. Three of his four grandparents were Irish. Among his family are the Ffrenches of Galway and Roscommon, the Lynches of Galway, the Woods of Sligo, and the Dillons of Roscommon, indeed these are the same family as Viscount Dillon who raised Dillon's Irish Brigade in France. So with an Irish mother and a half-Irish father, Gonville Bromhead was himself three-quarters Irish, a situation whereby he could, indeed should, be regarded as qualifying as being indisputably a very Irish Frenchman at Rorke's Drift.

The man who first mooted the merits of making a stand was Acting Assistant Commissary James Langley Dalton, a Roman Catholic born in the Parish of St. Andrews, Middlesex, London, in December 1831 to

Irish parents James and Susan Dalton. Verification of their exact origins in Ireland is difficult to ascertain, but a connection to the Westmeath-Longford area is likely. Red-haired and tall, James Dalton's physicality was as imposing as his experience was impressive, and his manner was authoritative.

B company, 2nd Battalion, 24th Foot arrived in South Africa during March 1878 and so had an involvement in what remained of the Ninth Cape Frontier War. The 24th, having its home depot established at Brecon, South Wales, in 1873 saw an increase in the number of Welsh men recruited into the regiment, more so to the 2nd Battalion than to the 1st, because the latter had been stationed overseas since that time. However it is a myth to believe Rorke's Drift was defended entirely by Welshmen, and like any unit of the Victorian era it had a liberal cross-section of English, Irish and Scotsmen. In fact, a more thorough examination than conducted heretofore reveals the Irish participation at Rorke's Drift – including native Irish-born, others born of Irish parents in Britain, and those with Irish names and connections – to be proportionately higher than considered heretofore, now most likely in the region of thirty individuals, of a total combined figure of English, Irish, Welsh, and Scot of 137 or so. Those native Irish-born were Surgeon Major James Henry Reynolds, Dublin, Assistant Commissary Walter Dunne, South Parish, Cork, Sergeant Henry Gallagher, Thurles Co. Tipperary, Privates James Bush, St John's, Dublin; Timothy Connors Killeaty, Co. Cork; James Dick, Islandmagee, Co. Antrim; James Hagan, Nenagh, Co. Tipperary; Thomas Lynch, Limerick; Michael Minehan, Castlehaven, Co. Cork; Augustus Morris, Dublin; Thomas Robinson, St Patrick's, Dublin; Michael Tobin, Windygap, Co. Kilkenny; Drummer Patrick Hayes, Newmarket, Co. Clare; Private Henry Turner, Ballsbridge, Dublin; Drummer Patrick Gagley, St Patrick's, Cork; John Manley, Cork; Garret Hayden, Dublin; and Michael Kiley, Mitchelstown, Co, Cork. Others born of Irish parents in Britain were Acting Assistant Commissary James Langley Dalton, born in London of parents most likely from the Westmeath-Longford area; Private John William Fielding, born in Abergavenny, Monmouthshire, Wales, of Cork City parents Michael Fielding and Margaret Godsil; and Corporal John 'Jack' Jeremiah Lyons born in Pontypool, Monmouthshire, Wales, of Cork parents John and Mary Lyons. Finally, those with Irish names and connections were Privates Thomas Buckley, Anthony Connors, John Fagan, John Murphy, Patrick Desmond, and William Herrigan, as well as storeman Louis Byrne and Private Michael McMahon, Army Hospital Corps.

Lieutenant Chard had tasked Lieutenant Henderson and his mounted body of a hundred men to go forward of Shiyane hill, act as early warning of the Zulu approach, engage in a delaying action, then return to the post to take up positions along the perimeter. They were not long gone when the ominous smattering of gunfire was heard; 'contact' with the Zulus had been made. Time was up. What exactly was coming or the numbers involved could only be guessed at. It was time to stand shoulder to shoulder, fight the fear, and face the danger. But that was not what Lieutenant Henderson's mounted party did. Having made brief contact with the Zulus they withdrew and kept on withdrawing, failing to rally around the post, and galloped away, making for the safety of Helpmakaar ten miles to the rear!

Lieutenant Henderson and a second man, Bob Hall, a meat contractor, momentarily reined in their mounts. Stating he could not control his men, Henderson then turned and rode after them. This sudden abandonment caused a panicked collapse of the courage of the Natal Native Contingent who also broke and spectacularly decamped, bounding over the mealie-bag barricades and fleeing. 'I am sorry to say,' reported Chard, 'that their officer [Captain George Stevenson], who had been doing good service getting his men to work, also deserted us.' Along with them went their

British NCOs. This betrayal was heartfelt, a blow which first shocked then infuriated those remaining, some of whom in their anger and outrage fired after them; one, a Corporal Anderson, was shot dead.

With the Zulus coming and the defenders diminishing, Chard had to improvise quickly, fearful of the now chillingly clear reality of the implications of the double defections,

The defenders, now numbering about 140, had to man a perimeter designed for 250. Should the Zulus mount a simultaneous attack on all sides at once, they might easily become overstretched; a fall-back barricade was needed, a line along which the perimeter could be contracted and the defenders concentrated. Chard instructed this to be made of biscuit boxes, two high, commencing at the left corner of the storehouse and running straight across the yard to the mealie-bag barricade. So if either building became compromised and had to be evacuated, either side of the new bisected perimeter could be better defended.

Amongst the brave band that remained standing was 'The Quiet Sergeant', Henry Gallagher from Killenaule, Co. Tipperary. A clerk on enlistment, he joined the British Army in Liverpool on 1874 and won rapid promotion because of his quickness to learn. He was to marry Caroline Maria Stanley and they were to have six children, his three sons all having careers in the army. He left for South Africa in February 1878 on the troopship *Himalaya*, arriving there in early March. With the 2nd/24th he was involved in the skirmishing which took place during April and May with Xhosa warriors in the Ninth Cape Frontier War. In January 1879 he was at Rorke's Drift as senior sergeant of B Company, 2nd/24th. He was placed along the south wall of the mealie-bag barricade situated between the wagons and the hospital, in charge of a section of 'shots' (sharp shooters).

The tiny garrison were on tenterhooks, the tension tangible, the fear obvious in their faces. Private Fred Hitch was placed on the hospital roof to look out for the Zulu assault force. Once they were sighted by him, he informed Sergeant Gallagher who then turned to the officers behind him and called out, 'Here they come as thick as grass and as black as thunder.'

Sergeant Henry Gallagher fighting with Zulu warrior.

(Illustration by Ray Fitzpatrick)

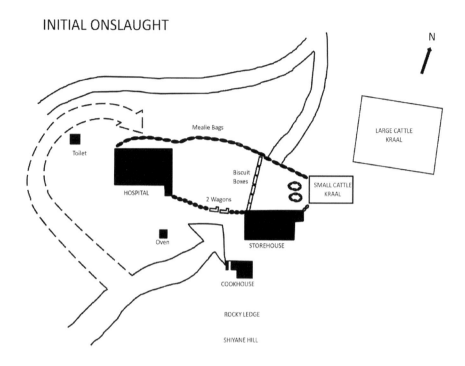

INITIAL ONSLAUGHT

N

Mealie Bags

LARGE CATTLE KRAAL

Toilet

Biscuit Boxes

SMALL CATTLE KRAAL

HOSPITAL

2 Wagons

Oven

STOREHOUSE

COOKHOUSE

ROCKY LEDGE

SHIYANE HILL

The initial attack by the Zulus on Rorke's Drift.

'THE FIRST RUSH'

On 22 January 1879 acting Assistant Commissary James Dalton found himself having to suggest, then supervise the physical strengthening of Rorke's Drift against the first rush of Zulu attack. An experienced ex-soldier, having served as a senior NCO, he was knowledgeable in African ways and knew that while offence was the most decisive type of military operation, defence was the stronger. He knew that there was no alternative; if they opted for disengagement and made a run for it, they would die. He knew that a strong-point perimeter security tied into a natural obstacle or critical terrain could present a defence without an exposed flank, which would cause difficulties for the Zulu as they would have no one point of attack or particular place they could encircle. This allowed the defenders to concentrate their mass, allowing a full 360 degree arc of fire, giving them an ability to repel an attack from any direction. The role of infantry on the battlefield was to close with and engage the enemy, but now they found themselves having to go on the defensive and hold a territorial objective. Although far from being an impenetrable bastion, Rorke's Drift had been prepared with good physical security, and now the time had come to secure it further with firepower. With the first appearance of the Zulu assault force, even though still at some far-off distance, Dalton encouraged his men to engage them far out in order to kill as many as possible as their attack advanced.

Dalton appreciated the penetrative power of the Martini-Henry rifle's .450 heavy-calibre bullet. Although still single shot, the workings of this then state-of-the-art rifle rendered it, by the standard of the time, an advanced rapid-firing, long-range rifle with deadly accuracy. In short, its 'stopping power' was phenomenal. With a nominal range of 1,000 yards, in the right hands it came into its own at 500 yards, made the ordinary firer look good at 300 yards and was a weapon-handler's dream thereafter. It took eight seconds to load, and the cocking-lever mechanism made for ease of handling, the firer pushing the unjacketed lead bullets into the breech with his thumb. It was known to have quite a 'kick' if the butt was incorrectly held and not sufficiently nestled against the shoulder. But held correctly or not, after the firing of multiple rounds the breech heated up and expanded, allowing black powder to flash black, which was exactly what happened with Sergeant Henry Gallagher whose right cheek and nose would bear the blue-black tattooing mark of the flash for the rest of his life.

It was the Ndluyengwe Regiment, made up of the young, fitter members of the *Undi* (Reserve) who came on first. And they came on fast, 500 to 600 of them, initially adopting the favoured crescent formation. Having fully swung around the base of the Shiyane hill, they first came fully into the defenders' view at the back (south) wall some 600 yards out. Changing stride and breaking formation, they went into open order, darting from cover to cover and crouching low, their shields at out-stretched arm's length in front of them. The Battle of Rorke's Drift was beginning. It was now 4.30pm but no one within the perimeter was checking their watches as their eyes, mesmerised, stayed peeled to the attacking Zulus, their hearts pounding, their mouths dry, each man amongst his comrades but still much alone with himself. Their momentary paralysis was suddenly shattered by Chard's barked order to 'open fire…independently at will'. There was a huge relief in firing off this first round; it steadied their nerves, they were now doing what a soldier knew how to do with the tool of his trade. Their first shots were high, wild, and did not register a hit. But they had done their job in settling themselves down, and those that followed began to find their mark. The Zulus first fast rush came on tactically, weaving and swerving behind any available cover and staying low to avoid the bullets. Those who were hit gave a little spring in the air before falling down flat, dead or dying. But the advance did not falter one bit. As Surgeon Reynolds remarked,

> *On they came at the same slow, slinging trot, their heads forward, their arms outspread, their bodies poised in a sort of aim at our mealie circus, and all in a dead silence. Here and there a black body doubled up and went writhing and bouncing in the dust; but the great host came steadily on…*

James Dalton was amongst the men of the back wall and his experience and encouragement ensured an effective steady rate of fire, but still the Zulus continued to close the gap. The nearer they got, the more confident they became; this first charge of the battle looked like it might end it quickly, and in their favour, the defenders' discipline and marksmanship proving no match for Zulu bravery. At fifty yards out, however, more of the defenders' guns came into play and arcs of fire from the store and the hospital were added to that coming from the back wall. Taking a sudden, voluminous increase of fire from the flanks and ever increasingly effective direct fire from the front, the Zulu warriors, amid rapidly mounting casualties, finally faltered. As Lieutenant Chard put it,

> *We opened fire on them, between five and six hundred yards, at first a little wild, but only for a short time . . . The men were quite steady, and*

the Zulus began to fall very quick. However, it did not seem to stop them at all . . . seemed that nothing would stop them, and they rushed on in spite of their heavy loss to within fifty yards of the wall, when they were takin in the flank by the fire from the end wall of the store building, and met with such a heavy direct fire from the mealie wall and the hospital at the same time that they were checked as if by magic.

Dalton, seeing the Zulus lose momentum and fall face down in the grass, clambered onto one of the wagons and in sheer exhilaration threw his hat at them. He had planned the defence and invigorated the defenders, and they had not flinched. It was a huge psychological victory; they had confronted their fears and had halted the Zulus' first headlong rush, and he had shown the way.

Having gone to ground, some of the attackers took cover around the abandoned cookhouse and ovens about thirty-five yards outside the perimeter and opened fire on the back wall from there. However, most of the attacking force had veered left around the outside of the hospital towards the front of the post, occupying the bushes fifty-five yards in front. Here the shrubbery and a conveniently placed five-foot-high stone wall which ran for a hundred yards gave advantageous cover. Hardly settling and regrouping within minutes, they made a determined dash, running rapidly up the less steep slope near the front corner of the hospital. The Zulus had found the weak spot. This attempted penetration had to be prevented, and the fighting became hand-to-hand, no quarter asked or given as bayonet met with spear. If time and space allowed, rifles were reloaded and fired. In one instance, a Zulu hand grabbed the bayonet of a hospital company private and, pushing his rifle aside, was poised with spear in hand to strike when he was suddenly shot by Dalton; he had raced over from the back wall along with Sergeant Henry Gallagher and some others to help Lieutenant Bromhead and Company Colour-

Sergeant Frank Bourke who with reinforcements were strengthening the defence to good effect. Several successive assaults had to be repulsed as the Zulu dead were mounting up.

Surgeon Reynolds described the initial rush and dash attacks as follows,

> *We opened fire on them from the hospital at 600 yards and, although the bullets ploughed through their midst and knocked over many, there was no check of alternation made in their approach. As they got nearer they became more scattered, but the bulk of them rushed for the hospital and the garden in front of it. We found ourselves quickly surrounded by the enemy with their strong force holding the garden and the shrubbery. From all sides, but especially the latter places, they poured on us a continuous fire, to which our men replied as quickly as they could reload their rifles.*

The battle was on, and already bloody. The Zulus had approached around the base of Shiyane hill, rushed to the south wall, were defeated and deflected into making a dash for the hospital corner. The Zulus had advanced and attacked, but their first efforts had been contained. It was then that the Zulu main body arrived. The battle was about to become a whole lot bloodier.

'FIX BAYONETS'

The human condition looks for certainty; in combat there is no such thing. There is only now, there is who is beside you, and what is in front of you. The fighting becomes compartmentalised; your perspective narrows, becomes myopic, you have to deal with the danger nearest to you. The battle line at Rorke's Drift was the mealie-bag barricade and the brutal actuality was kill or be killed.

Much of what occurred at Rorke's Drift was instinctive, an inborn impulse honed by training and an inherent intuition to do what was necessary to survive. Concentration was paramount, the focusing of all one's attention and energies to fight. The defenders and attackers had come to close-quarter blows, ferocious, fiery, and fierce. What became apparent early on was the Zulu respect for 'the lunger', the twenty-two inch bayonet fixed to the Martini-Henry rifle. The combined reach of rifle and bayonet together elongated its length to nearly six foot, double that of the Zulu spear. Standing behind the barricades, rifle and bayonet in hand on top of the high rocky overhang, granted the defenders a favourable position. The defenders' bayonet thrusts made the Zulus flinch and become uncertain, more so than the lethal effect of the bullet. The Zulus had made a leisurely approach to Rorke's Drift from

Siege of Rorke's Drift by W.H. Dugan.

Isandlwana, pausing on the high ground above the Buffalo River to take snuff, powdered tobacco laced with hemp extract, which they believed made them immune to gunfire, if not immortal, but the bayonet still frightened them. They were, however, not so discouraged to the point of not pursuing what they had come to Rorke's Drift to do, to 'eat up, the red soldiers'. Behind the mealie-bag barricades, soldiers from England, Ireland, Wales, and Scotland had already met and held their first attack. But now the Zulus were closing in upon them. The first fevered rushes had just been fended off when the Zulu main body of the *Undi* (Reserve), comprising the older senior warriors of the Zulu – the Thulwana, iNdlondho, and Dloko – manoeuvred into position, veering similarly around the hospital and joining the iNduyengwe in the dense shrubbery in front of the hospital, preparing to renew the attack on the hospital veranda with increased intensity. Some of this main body of Zulus had, however, broken away and taken up position on the rocky terrace on Shiyane hill more than 300 yards to the rear of the post, from where they were able to maintain a hail of fire right down onto the post. They were not able, however, to make this advantage a decisive one because of the distance and their obsolete flintlocks and out-dated percussion rifles, allied with poor quality shot and black powder. The defenders along the back (south) barricade, who were already keeping the Zulu attack on the back of the post pinned down, also returned fire very effectively under the direction of Sergeant Henry Gallagher, now once more back in position, thus somewhat mitigating the threat. Notwithstanding, the Zulus could and would cause concern among the posts defenders with dangerous fires directed from there.

'Usuthu' came the war cry as the Zulus rose up out of the cover and charged forward. Met by a devastating close-range fuselage from the defenders, there were plenty more to take the place of the fallen. No chance to reload, the bayonet came into play. The Zulus pressed forward, the defenders met them head-on. They had to, as any gaps that arose would be quickly exploited by the Zulus instantly pouring through the break, the hundreds more behind following to quickly seal the defenders' fate. So the defensive effort had always to be here and now, successful, and maintained. With the attackers looking to breach the mealie-bag barricade and the defenders using 'cold steel' against overwhelming odds, courage, concentration, and constant physical exertion were called for on both sides. The numerical advantage weighed heavily in favour of the Zulus, suggesting time and attrition alone must surely decide the matter.

It is important to appreciate how critical the rocky overhang running along the front of the post was, providing a sturdy natural barrier against the Zulu attack. It was only a few yards high but when topped by the mealie-bag barricade it created a formidable obstruction. It did, however, offer the Zulus the benefit of dead ground immediately below the rock, where they could huddle down, then leap up to fire at the

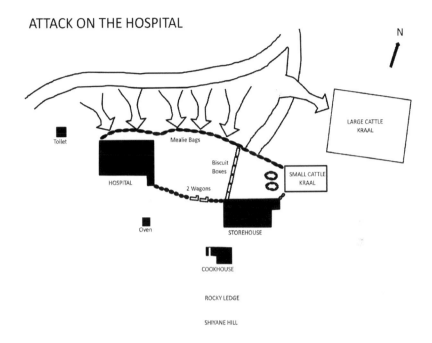

ATTACK ON THE HOSPITAL

N

LARGE CATTLE KRAAL

Toilet

Mealie Bags

Biscuit Boxes

HOSPITAL

2 Wagons

SMALL CATTLE KRAAL

Oven

STOREHOUSE

COOKHOUSE

ROCKY LEDGE

SHIYANE HILL

The Zulu attack on the hospital building.

defenders at close range. Collective Zulu fire from the rocky overhang shelf, from the shrubbery, and from the further out rocky ledge on the slope of Shiyane hill, together with the defenders' return fire, meant there was a lot of noise, smoke, and lead in the air, both incoming and outgoing. Inevitably, some incoming struck home, and the casualties began to mount within the perimeter. Proportionately, the loss in terms of defenders put 'out of action' was harder felt than among the vastly numerically superior attacking force. The first Irishman to be killed was Louis Byrne, a civilian volunteer serving as a store man with the Commissary Department, who went to the aid of a wounded Corporal Scannell (Natal Native Contingent) to give him a drink of water; in the course of doing so, he was struck through the head and killed.

The cry of 'Usuthu' filled the air again as the Zulus flung themselves at the barricade; each time it seemed as if the defenders would buckle under the onslaught. Desperate and repeated attacks were met with a steady and deliberate defence. The Zulu attack extended now along most of the north wall barricade and it crashed home again and again as wave after wave was ordered forward. All it would take was for the defence somewhere, anywhere, along the line to lose its cohesion, become scattered and confused, and the already grim hand-to-hand fighting would come to its gruesome conclusion. They were, quite literally, fighting for their lives. The effect of the rocky overhang running along the length of the north wall restricted the frontage along which they could fight and thus prevented Dabulamanzi's Zulus hurling themselves all at once onto the barricade. The attackers came on in their hundreds, not thousands, and as a result their rushes were met and checked, man to man. A type of pattern in the deadly ebb of and flow of the battle began to become apparent. Lieutenant Chard described the fighting as follows,

A series of desperate assaults was made on the hospital, and extending from the hospital, as far as the bush reached; but each was most splendidly met and repulsed by our men, with the bayonet. Each time as the attack was repulsed by us, the Zulus close to us seemed to vanish in the brush, those some little distance off keeping up a fire all time. Then as if moved by a single impulse, they rose up in the bush as thick as possible, rushing madly up to the wall (some of them being already close to it), seizing where they could the muzzles of our men's rifles, or their bayonets, and attempting to use their assegais and to get over the wall. A rapid rattle of fire from our rifles, stabs with the bayonet, and in a few moments the Zulus were driven back, disappearing in the bush as before, and keeping up their fire. A brief interval and the attack would be made again, and repulsed in the same manner. Over and over again this happened, our men behaviour with the greatest coolness and gallantry.

Acting Assistant Commissary James Langley Dalton was there, leading with his impressively felt bearing and presence. Dalton's inspirational example galvanised and uplifted many, particularly the young defenders. Chard went on to report,

> *Our fire at the time of these rushes was very rapid – Mr. Dalton dropping a man each time he fired his rifle, while Bromhead and myself used our revolvers.*

The revolver in use was the Tranter .450cap. Bromehad was later on to arm himself also with a Martini-Henry rifle.

The fragmentary nature of battle, particularly when it is close, often means the participants, even those in command, have a disjointed, discontinuous view of the fighting. Chard reported,

> *It is impossible for one individual to see all, but I particularly myself noticed the behaviour of Colour-Sergeant Bourne 24th, Sergeant Williams 24th, Corporal Schiess NNC, Corporal Lyons 24th [Irish], Private McMahon AHC [Irish], Private Roy, Deacon, Bush [Irish], Cole, Jenkins, 24th, and many others. . .*

Evident also was the attentive medical care administered by Surgeon Reynolds who had established an improvised first-aid station on the veranda of the storehouse. He repeatedly entered into the fray, at great personal risk to himself, to tend to those requiring treatment. Improvising, he carried out 'running repairs' on the hoof, patching up the many recipients of minor wounds, cuts, and bruises, as few escaped completely unscathed. In so extreme a situation, an indefinite struggle of high intensity, the physical demands were huge: the exertion, the heat, the profuse sweating, dehydration and exhaustion, the necessity to put yourself in a position of being constantly exposed to danger, all took its toll. But for now, it was all about now, and just surviving to the next now.

What had a direct bearing on this was the closeness of the contest, and even when separated they were not that far distant and remained engaged in the fire fight. 'Heavens! They rained lead on us at the distance of a cricket pitch or two...' Reynolds wrote. 'We stood up face to face, white men and black, and blazed at each other till nightfall.' But it was the nature of the natural rocky ledge overhang running the substantive length of the north wall, albeit only a few yards high, that dramatically increased the effectiveness of the defence. This topographical feature, along with the positive effect of Dalton on the defenders' morale and the technologically advanced Martini-Henry rifle and bayonet, could all three be regarded as 'force multipliers', as they all significantly increased the combat potential of the defenders.

In front of the hospital the rock outcrops gave way to a more gentle graduation in the slope of the ground. The much put-upon double defence line here was stretched too thin, granting the Zulus the opportunity to exploit into this area. A series of deadly assaults was made towards the hospital. The defenders, without panic, acceded the ground to them at the north-west corner. The Zulus had seized the weak point in front of the hospital. At this point Lieutenant Chard was tempted to collapse the perimeter back to the biscuit-box barricade bisecting the compound, but it would mean leaving those in the hospital in difficulty. Instead, he sought to contain the penetration by quickly erecting a short barricade between the innermost or front-right hospital corner with the north wall barricade – this was to become known as the 'dog leg' – behind which he placed a line of defenders able to fire into the hospital compound area. Those within the hospital itself were barricaded inside and firing out through loopholes, so while the area in front of the hospital had become physically abandoned it was still controlled by the defenders' fire. While this was progressing the pressure along the entirety of the north wall was intensified. The Zulus, however, unable to make further headway despite heroic athletic leaps onto the mealie-bag barricade, only to be summarily shot or bayoneted by the defenders, extended their line of assault further along the barricade line to in front of the storehouse, specifically to the second weak spot. A wagon track ran towards the storehouse here through the rocky overhang ledge. Blocked by mealie bags, it was a less discouraging prospect from an attackers' viewpoint, and they made for it. Clambering up onto the front mealie-bag barricade all along the line, they concurrently made a determined drive on the barricade directly in front of the storehouse where the path to the building passed through the rock ledge. It was a serious assault, and for a moment it looked likely they would get in over the wall there because of the tenacity of their attack. Lieutenants Chard and Bromhead, each with an additional small group of two or three, helped those already there to maintain a sufficiently rapid fire to tip the balance and repel the attack. Chard was aware that he who defends everything defends nothing; they were coming under too much pressure, and continuing to defend the full perimeter was risking the ever-increasing likelihood of it becoming punctured. He wrote,

> *At about 6.00pm, the enemy extending their attack further to their left, I feared seriously would get in over our wall behind the biscuit boxes. I ran back with 2 or 3 men to this part of the wall and was immediately joined by Bromhead with 2 or 3 more. The enemy struck to this assault most tenaciously, and on their repulse, and retiring to the bush, I called all the men inside the retrenchment...*

Assistant Commissary Walter Dunne building the 'Redoubt'.

(Illustration by Ray Fitzpatrick)

Surgeon Reynolds account of this action read as follows,

> *Again and again the Zulus pressed forward and retreated, until at last they forced themselves so daringly and in such numbers, as to climb over the mealie sacks in front of the hospital, and drove the defenders from there behind a trenchment of biscuit boxes, hastily formed with such judgement and forethought by Lieutenant Chard. A heavy fire from behind it was resumed with renewed confidence, and with little confusion or delay, checking successfully the natives, and permitting a semi-flank fire from another part of the hanger to play on them destructively!*

The same number of men were now required to protect a smaller area, and being more closely packed together they were better able to defend themselves. They were also better protected by the storehouse blocking enemy fires from Shiyane Hill and elsewhere. The fire that they could bring to bear from behind the biscuit-box barricade prevented the Zulus from forcing their way into the yard. It was not all good news though; in trading space for security, they had ceded control of being able to keep the Zulus away from the hospital building, and surrendered the immediate areas on the other side (lee side) of the front and rear barricades behind which they Zulus could shelter and mass together to spring up and rush them, or fire at even shorter ranges. A steady volume of fire, however, kept the abandoned yard free and supported to some extent those remaining within the hospital building.

On hearing the shouts for ammunition resupply from the now beleaguered defenders of the hospital, Surgeon Reynolds decided to take it upon himself to assist them. Heaping up packets of ammunition into his arms folded like the shape of a bread basket, he dashed across the yard, now 'no man's territory', to the hospital's gable-end high window and passed the packets through. For the most part unseen by the Zulus, he was, however, in plain sight of one who fired. The bullet struck a hole in his helmet but missed his head, and he made it back safely to the storehouse veranda. The garrison had not only his bravery to marvel at, but also his good fortune.

Now after six o'clock, the fighting having raged for almost two hours, the battle lines had been redrawn. The defensive perimeter had shrank, the hospital defenders isolated, but, for the most part, the Zulus had been held at bay. But there was much fighting to be done yet, and the Irish would be in the thick of it.

RIFLE-BUTTS, BULLETS, AND BAYONETS

Opportunity is only as great as the use made of it. In the circumstances now prevailing, with the defenders forced to occupy a small area and the hospital fallen, the Zulus most likely felt that total success would be shortly achievable. And if complete victory had eluded them so far, what they had in the moment was enough, they may have thought, to see them prevail. This new situation, however, demanded to be exploited by stepping up the level of engagement. With darkness descending, the Zulu attacks became increasingly aggressive and more audacious, the defence more desperate, the fighting more frenzied and sustained. The Zulu pressure on the front barricade in the foreground of the storehouse was concentrated, cold-blooded, and cruel. It was designed to crush conclusively and completely. Yet the defence would not crumble. Murderous close-quarter fire fights, savage and unsparing hand-to-hand struggles, a new brutality evident, untamed and unimagined – every action in the fight was a moment of truth in itself. Nonetheless the repeated Zulu attacks were being repelled despite the increasing number of fatalities and wounded.

The best-laid battle plans rarely survive the first shots and so too with the retrenchment enclosure, the fall-back position. Crucial but not impregnable, it soon became clear that the angle between the front wall and the line of biscuit boxes was now the most vulnerable part of the perimeter. These were becoming ever increasingly hard times for the defenders, those in the exposed corner being steadily shot down. Inevitably present and still immense in defence was Dalton. Chard said of him, 'While firing from behind the biscuit boxes, Dalton, who had been using his rifle with deadly effect. . . by his quickness and coolness had been the means of saving many men's lives. . .' However, not all the lives were saveable, and some died horribly from ghastly wounds. One of the most hideous was to occur to Private Nicholas who received a shot in the head, which sprayed the grey matter of his brain over those fighting beside him. Also shot in the head and killed was Private Cole, the bullet passing through and striking Private James Bushe from Dublin on the nose, who survived. Irishman John Fagan unfortunately when shot did not. Others would share a similar fate, and although the defenders exacted a high cost in return, the attackers continued to come charging in. This was the Zulus' most determined effort yet. Each assault, however, was met with a matched unwavering doggedness. Because of the close proximity of the point from where the attacks were launched, just below the overhanging rocky ledge, there was only time for the defenders to let off one round of fire before they had to resort to the use of the bayonet and the rifle-butt. This was hard fighting, and without close attention to what was happening an irreversible turning point in the violent struggle could all too easily be reached, taking them to the cusp of a rout that would be ruthlessly exposed in an agonisingly short time. If adversity really does reveal character, nothing exposed it with more intensity that this seething cauldron. It was a matter of guts and grit to withstand the Zulus' unbridled aggression. Time and time again they rushed the north wall barricade, those not shot down leaping up onto the mealie-bags; the Martini-Henrys if quickly reloaded would respond with shuddering effect, and then 'the lunger' would come into play, the defenders' bayonets jabbing forward to dispatch those remaining, only for another wave to arrive and be driven back. Then it was time to reload, fire at the next oncoming onslaught, avoid being cudgelled by a blow from a club or skewered by a spear or cut by a blade. And on it went, attack and defence.

The light from the fire of the burning hospital building was now proving advantageous to the defenders. While the darkness, now well and truly descended, brought no lessening in the ferocity of the Zulus' attacks, the flames leaping from the hospital's thatched roof provided a halo of light for the defenders to fire by. Emerging out of the shrubbery and the darkness, the Zulus entered the illuminated area surrounding the post's perimeter and thus presented themselves as clear visual targets for the defenders to pour bullets into both as they attacked and retreated. The burning debris sent sparks propelling into the night sky, making the battle space about fifty yards or so around the building a well-lit one. The Zulus made several attempts to set fire to the thatched roof of the storehouse. The defenders inside at its rear wall fired through the loopholes at the would-be arsonists and they ran out of the shadows into the light, cutting them off before they could set the storehouse ablaze.

The defenders showed immense bravery. A Corporal Ferdinand Schiess from Switzerland, a member of the Natal Native Contingent who was a patient in the hospital suffering from blisters, on seeing the struggle continuing at the exposed angle of the biscuit box and mealie-bag wall, decided to join in the defence of the perimeter and put himself in grave danger by creeping out from behind the mealie-bag wall and leaping onto the top of the barricade where he shot and bayoneted three attackers crouching below the rocky ledge along the front of the post. Another notable action was undertaken by Private Fred Hitch who saw that Lieutenant Bromhead was about to be 'run though' with an assegai

NIGHT ATTACKS

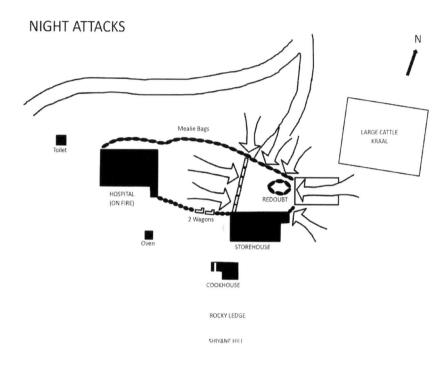

NIGHT ATTACKS

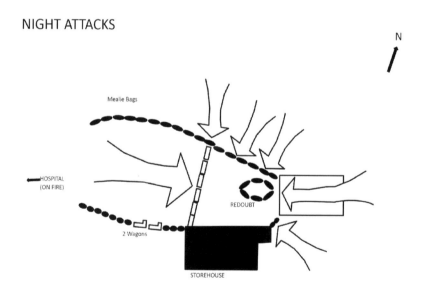

Night attacks by the Zulus.

and put his unloaded rifle to this shoulder and shouted at the attacker to get his attention, who then dropped back over the barricade. Not long after, he himself was engaged in a hand-to-hand encounter and seeing another Zulu pointing his rifle directly at him, unable to defend himself further, waited for the impact of the bullet, which struck him in the shoulder, shattering it. The Zulu came forward to finish him but this time Bromhead intervened and saved him. Surgeon Reynolds took forty bone fragments from Hitch's wound. Returning to the fray and borrowing Bromhead's revolver, Hitch continued to account for attacking Zulus. When he was unable to continue fighting he contributed by passing out ammunition to his comrades until he fainted because of loss of blood. Also ferrying ammunition around the perimeter, having been previously wounded, was Corporal Alan Williams. He had received a bullet wound to his arm while firing from the biscuit-box barricade close to the storehouse and the lee of the south wall. He and Hitch had paired up as a team, each using his one serviceable arm to distribute the much-needed ammunition.

A defence needs depth so that it not easily overrun if breached. Chard's defence, however, had no space left to build it in, so he chose to go upwards instead, and the means to do so were immediately to hand. Two huge piles of mealie-bags stood, undistributed around the perimeter, right in front of the storehouse veranda. These, Chard suggested, could be used to elevate riflemen to a higher level, providing an additional layer of fire over the heads of those fighting along the perimeter. Chard was to report after,

We converted two large heaps of mealie bags into a sort of redoubt, which gave a second line of fire all round, and formed a strong position to hold and rally around in case of the store-building hut had to be abandoned, or the enemy broke through elsewhere. Assistant Commissary Dunne

worked hard at this; from his height, being a tall man, he was much exposed, in addition to the fact that the heaps were high above our walls and that most of the Zulu bullets went high.

Walter Dunne from Cork undertook the work with a team of four or five others, taking mealie-bags off the top of each heap, in-filling the gap between, blending both into one, then working from the top centre to create and all-round rampart rim on the outside edge. Dunne hmself described the process as follows,

Chard decided to form a sort of redoubt of mealie-bags, where a last stand could be made. We laboured at this till we dropped with exhaustion, but succeeded in building it up to about eight feet on the outside, and here the wounded were brought for protection. It was hard work, for the bags of mealie weighed 200lbs each. Overhead, the small birds disturbed from their nests by the turmoil and the smoke flew hither and thither confusedly.

With bullets and assegais flying, he was indeed fortunate not to be injured.

Dalton, who had also deliberately put himself in harm's way and seemed about to cheat death, was not so fortunate. Chard recounted that Dalton,

. . . was shot though the body. I was standing near him at the time, and he handed me his rifle so coolly that I had no idea until afterwards of how severely he was wounded. He waited quite patiently for me to take the cartridges he had left out of his pockets. We put him inside our mealie-bag redoubt, building it up around him.

Chaplain Smith was to say of the incident,

Mr Dalton, who is a tall man, was continually going around the barricades, fearlessly exposing himself and cheering the men, and using his own rifle most effectively. But whiles firing at the attackers he was shot and badly wounded in the right shoulder. He was unable to continue and laid down behind a pile of mealie-bags.

Surgeon Reynolds, who treated his wound, wrote,

The bullet entered about half an inch above the middle of the clavicle, then made its escape posteriorly at the lowest border of the trapezius muscle. The course taken was curious, regularly running round the shoulder and down the back, escaping all the important structures. After the slough came away the usual tenax was applied. The whole field medical equipment, having been captured by the enemy at Isandlwana, I had no antiseptic to use. I thought of quinine, which I knew was a wonderful preserver of animal tissues, and used a solution of that, experimenting in this case. It seemed to answer, as the wounds got on well after being injected several times with it.

Unable to make headway against the north wall, the Zulus, while continuing to assault it, changed their main point of attack to the far eastern end of the perimeter, to the drystone walled cattle-kraal, the furthest point from the blazing hospital. They were seeking the cover of darkness from where to mount their rushing charges. The cloak of night was to be their ally. Ordinarily, the Zulus considered night a time of *umnyama*, a time of inauspicious omen, populated with dark spiritual forces. Yet it was the very time they chose to ramp up their already intensive attack in search of a break-in. There was a great deal of fight left in the Zulus. Could the defenders continue to hold out against sustained pressure? Or would it prove a time of *umnyama* for them?

*Private John William Fielding making
'mouse-holes' in the hospital building wall.*

(Illustration by Ray Fitzpatrick)

FIGHTING FEAR

To be frightened and still be brave, that is real courage. And that courage was exactly what the defenders required as the Zulus in overwhelming numbers prepared to break into the hospital and turn it into a slaughterhouse. Fear was understandable, but it had also to be countered unless it overcame and broke the spirit, just as it had done with Henderson's men. As night fell rapidly – the African twilight is not one that lingers – the defenders, peering into the near darkness, must have wondered with trepidation and barely subdued panic about what was coming next. The real battleground was deep within each man's being, and each had to struggle not to come apart at the seams in order to cling to life itself as long as one could.

In the hurried preparation of the post's defensive measures, the decision was taken not to evacuate the hospital. Surgeon Reynolds discerned that eight patients were unfit for carrying arms, their infirmities and injuries preventing them from functioning independently. Some twenty or so of the more able-bodied convalescent patients were issued with Martini-Henry rifles and distributed throughout to contribute towards the defence of the hospital itself, the storehouse, and the perimeter. In addition, six members of B company were assigned to directly support the hospital building. Furniture had been stacked up and jammed against window and door frames to impede entry; these were barricaded with biscuit-boxes and mealie-bags; and the walls were loop-holed to fire through. The hospital building's layout was not conducive to free-flowing internal movement. In some rooms individual access doors opened outwardly, allowing entry and exit externally only. Internal access and circulation was confined, restricted by a confusing mixture of hotchpotch renovations over the years. Some rooms were small, enclosed, and now in the fast-fading light of sunset, becoming claustrophobic.

Originally the building was Jim Rorke's dwelling house, it's internal layout later rearranged by the Surtees family to accommodate two family units separately under the one roof. Only hours beforehand it had been improvised into one of two strong points, anchoring firmly in place the post's perimeter defence. It had withstood the initial onslaught of the first rush of Zulus, and had maintained the integrity of its defence in the fighting since, but now, following the garrison's withdrawal behind the biscuit-box barricade bisecting the compound, it had become detached, its defenders set apart. They were now having to fend off independently the attentions of hundreds of Zulus poised to pounce at sundown.

What then exactly had those inside the hospital building to do? Its very defence had been decided against, yet its physical structure was the only defence they had against the attacking Zulus massing outside, a defence in all likelihood to be short-lived. Their aim therefore was to get themselves and those incapacitated patients from danger to safety; in short, to evacuate. They had somehow to effect an escape, to evade and elude the Zulus. If they dared defy the dangers, it would have to be an audacious attempt, and they would need to fight their fear to find a way out of an impossible situation. Low on ammunition, largely unsupported by those across the compound behind the biscuit-box barricade, and almost completely surrounded by hundreds of Zulus, they were, as one of those defending the hospital building, Private Henry Hook from

Gloucestershire, put it, 'pinned like rats in a hole.'

Their predicament was actually worse than that, because the Zulus were literally adding flame to the defenders' already very difficult situation. They had set fire to the building's thatched roof, and the damp straw, for now, was beginning to burn slowly with smoke but no flame. It would not take long, however, before the smouldering thatched roof would fully ignite and the building would become a furnace consuming those left inside.

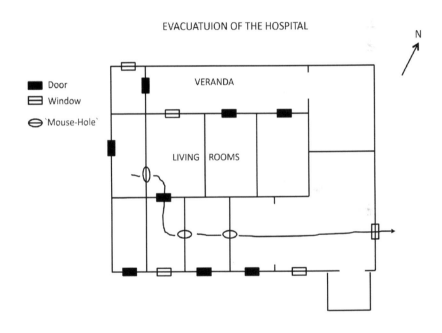

Evacuation of the hospital.

The building's layout meant the defenders were not a congregated collective, but rather a divided defence of small groups of twos and threes, maybe even a single soldier, per room, separated and isolated from each other, facing the terror of impossible odds and the likely prospect of a horrible death. Flight was their only real option but they would have to fight for this opportunity. The Zulus massed around the building and on the veranda would soon force the door and gain access, but they would have to go room by room to seek their prey. It would soon become a confused, disorienting melee with darkness, smoke, cries, shrieks, a manic merciless real-life melodrama, unrestrained and unforgiving. Those who could fight, would; those who could not, would immediately die, pierced open by spears or clubbed to death.

'The Zulus are swarming all over the place. They've dragged Joseph Williams out and killed him,' Private John William Fielding (born in Wales of parents from Cork city) called out as he hastily entered the room in which Private Alfred Henry Hook was. He and Williams had been in a room at the western gable-end wall with five patients, one of whom was Irishman 'Billy' William Horrigan. They were firing through loopholes despite the efforts of some of the Zulus outside attempting to grab hold of their rifle muzzles. The Zulus were desperately trying to force in the external door, and when those inside saw the door beginning to give, with no internal access door to the remainder of the building, they had desperately to find an alternative way out. With Billy Horrigan and Joseph Williams maintaining the fight, the latter having accounted for many dead Zulus, Fielding fortuitously found the pickaxe they had previously used to prepare the loopholes and began smashing a hole in the partition dividing wall, which easily gave way as it was made of thin mud-clay bricks. With the pickaxe and bayonets, all together made a hole at floor level big enough to squeeze through. These were called 'mouse-holes' and by such means they were able to retreat room by room along the rear of the hospital building. The Zulus pursued them vigorously and viciously. In order to buy time for Fielding to 'mouse-hole' frenetically through further walls, then drag the incapacitated patients through, Henry Hook would courageously stage a staunch rear-guard defence of the previous 'mouse-hole', keeping the Zulus in check with bullets and bayonet, before rushing through it himself. By the making and defending of these hurriedly excavated exits through the insubstantial interior walls, Fielding and Hook together managed to save the lives of those patients who were unable to save themselves. It was a struggle within a struggle.

Not all the patients had made it out of the western gable-end room, and a third Irishman, Private Garret Hayden, D Company 2nd/24th, who had enlisted in Dublin, was vigorously hauled outside and butchered. He was stabbed sixteen times. His stomach was twice cut open with violent, sweeping spear strokes and one of his cheeks was completely sliced off.

Meanwhile, those defenders in other parts of the hospital building, with the fire beginning to take firm hold in the thatched roof, decided to take their chances in the darkness and, after judging a lull in the fighting, broke out of the burning building into the compound. They went over the mealie-bags out into the bush and shrubbery, hoping to remain there unnoticed, or headed towards the biscuit-box barricade. Some, amazingly, made it to safety, but others did not. Irishman 'Billy' Horrigan had perished alongside Joseph Williams, the man he had fought beside.

Privates Hook and Fielding continued to make their way through more walls in order to reach the eastern-end gable wall, pulling and pushing the patients and defending against the following Zulus. This was not an easy undertaking a demanding a determination and nerve. Making it through into the last room, they found William and Robert Jones defending themselves and five other patients. The Joneses, not related, who had been defending for some time, were out of ammunition despite Surgeon Reynolds' earlier gallant resupply effort; the Zulus, aware of this cessation of fire, were now busily attempting to barge their way through the outer door. The Joneses put their shoulders to the door, pressing their body weight against it in order to prevent entry. The Zulus changed tack and, using their spears, they splintered the door, only for the Joneses to stand their ground and bayonet them as they appeared. This, however, they could not do indefinitely, so Privates Hook and Fielding had to use these scarce moments to get the patients out through the high window as fast as they could. Fielding went out first and, with Hook inside, together they helped the patients through the window into the compound yard. The evacuation attempt thus far had been very fraught, but now in the 'no man's land' that the yard had become, matters were even more fraught. The Zulus were crouched behind the mealie-bags on both sides, the south wall only yards distant, the north wall not a whole lot further. The escapees had now to run a gauntlet, exposed to short-range flying lead and spears.

Inauspiciously, the first man down was targeted by a Zulu who sprinted out from behind the 'dog-leg' barricade and speared him in the back, he in turn being shot down by those behind the biscuit-box barricade, who now gave support to the fleeing patients by firing on the mealie-bag positions and keeping the Zulus in check. One by one the patients dropped down from the window and made it as fast as they could across the yard to find safety in the storehouse. Not all were able to be swift; those unable to run, walked, those unable to walk, crawled. More than twenty patients made it to safety; by rights, no one should have made it at all. It was an extraordinary feat. The hospital defenders had brought out patients that would otherwise have been hacked to pieces. The defenders had been frightened, but stayed brave, and in doing so displayed rare courage.

'DO OR DIE'

The hastily constructed mealie-bag defensive emplacement, the redoubt ('a place of retreat'), was immediately manned when ready by a party of defenders to function as intended, to preserve their position for the duration of the conflict. The riflemen placed on this, the post's final protective position, were raised above the heads of those in front defending the barricades and were now able to bring additional firepower to bear wherever the perimeter was most in danger of collapse. The only thing was, the perimeter was constantly at risk everywhere, all along the north wall in front of the storehouse and now the adjacent cattle-kraal.

Among those on the redoubt was 'the Quiet Sergeant', Henry Gallagher from Co. Tipperary. Along with all those around him he had to maintain an almost continuous rate of fire since late afternoon; now, four hours later, repeated 'volley' and 'independent firing' had made the barrels of their Martini-Henry rifles become very hot. In the darkness they could see the barrels almost glowing red. Sergeant Gallagher had to tear the sleeve of his tunic to wrap around the barrel to stop his hand burning. Other ill effects of this relentless frequent firing were the black powder 'flash-backs' from the expanded breech and an increase in 'kick-back' recoil, bruising the shoulder. Also, the softening of the cartridges thumbed into the hot breech chambers caused the barrel to 'foul' through black gunpowder grit building up on the inside grooves of the barrel and the cartridge to jam on extraction. To remedy such 'stoppages', immediate action drills were second nature to a trained soldier; however, both the degree of frequency of this occurring and the urgency of the situation were not. Nonetheless, they worked away with their ram rods or pen-knives until the weapon was clear and ready to be brought back into action.

For a soldier manning the barricades, whenever his rifle jammed and there was little or no time to clear it before another rush of Zulus had to be met head-on, the three-sided bayonet proved a fine weapon. Some bayonets, however, were made of poor quality, and became twisted and badly bent. A jammed rifle with a bent bayonet was not an ideal weapon to have when encountering a Zulu onslaught. But then, the rifle's butt could be brought into play; in desperate circumstances, a disciplined soldier will use whatever is to hand.

For the most part, however, the rifles fired and the bayonets remained unbroken. Indeed, the bayonet on the Martini-Henry was a big bonus, its reach combined with the driving force of the soldier's lunge behind it meant some terrible thrusts were given. One such killing thrust was made by Private Michael Minehan from Castlehaven, Co. Cork. Son of Jeremiah Minehan and Johanna Hourihane, he was brought up in a modest cottage on land connected to Castlehaven's Glebe House. A groomsman on enlistment in Bandon into the 24th Regiment, he gave his age as 19, when in fact he was not long 18, to avoid being paid 'boy's wages'. It is unlikely that prior to joining the army he would have known his near neighbour Nevill Coghill (then aged 12), and less likely still to have mixed socially with him in the tiny village of Castletownshend; however, here they were together, soldiering in the same battalion in South Africa – Lieutenant Coghill already dead in his attempt with Melville to 'save the colours' of the 24th from Isandlwana, Michael Minehan fighting for his life at Rorke's Drift. The Zulus' main focus of attack at this point was concentrated on the eastern end of the post's perimeter, through the cattle-kraal. Initially the defenders occupied the entirety of the shoulder-high, dry-stone-walled kraal. Within was an interior wall partition at the midway point. Lined along the length of the far-off wall, the defenders faced a series of spirited assaults. Running towards them, looming out of the darkness at close range, the Zulu warriors made determined attacks, rattling assegais on their shields and chanting 'Usuthu, Usuthu, Usuthu', an old tribal war cry, its literal meaning 'fat cow', used to describe the name of the distinctive cattle of the Zulu royal clan, but in this specific context meant to espouse a chant of 'Power, Power, Power'. With a mental and physical forcefulness, they became increasingly frenzied and their resulting vigorous onslaught yielded the desired result in driving the defenders, Private Michael Minehan among them, from the exterior wall through the interior partition to the near wall. After they had re-established their firing line along this rearmost kraal wall, Private Minehan took up position at its corner and continued to fight from there. Suddenly, he felt a tug on his leg and looking down he saw a hand coming out from a heap of straw. A Zulu had stealthily slipped into the kraal and moved unobserved through and was now attempting to haul down Minehan. The West Cork man reacted quickly and skewered his attacker to the ground with his bayonet.

Above him, Sergeant Henry Gallagher was among those defenders in the redoubt, the perimeter defenders' 'overwatch', who were able to pour down support fire and together with those on the rear wall kept the Zulus pinned down. The defenders had regained the initiative, they had again acted to forestall the Zulu plan of attack. The situation was reaching stalemate. Thus far the defenders had out-thought and out-fought the Zulus. Dalton, Chard, and Bromhead had anticipated in defence what the Zulus would next do in attack. They had met the initial onslaught head-on and continued a determined defence against the subsequent extremely heavy attacks over the previous five hours or so. But still there was fight left in the Zulus; they still enjoyed the advantage of overwhelming numbers, had attacked ferociously over a sustained period, and their ardour remained intact. One more rush, concentrated, heavy, and sustained, would, they believed, achieve the much-wanted break-in and swamp the defence. Their war cry was heard again, alerting the defenders of another direct frontal assault against the barricades. It was do or die. It was all guns blazing again in defence, and all to good effect because the company-sized infantry square, concentrated and barricaded, did not flinch. Adding to this furious gunfire was the fire of Second Corporal Michael McMahon who early in the fight, despite being a member of the Army Medical Corps, had acquired a rifle and had joined in the defence. It was most likely his weapon that had been grabbed by a Zulu earlier inside the hospital barricade, yanking him off balance, and he was about to be driven through with an assegai when Dalton swiftly intervened and shot the attacker. No doubt shaken and relieved all at once, he returned to the fight and was fighting still.

The cattle-kraal proved to be a stumbling block for the Zulus. In their efforts to clamber over the outside wall they were exposed, and full advantage was taken by the defenders. Those who succeeded in getting beyond the wall had to do likewise with the partition wall positioned midway, only at closer range, and the defenders executed maximum advantage from this obstacle in combination with their gunfire. The Zulu attack petered out; fire control had won over fighting enthusiasm. And then, a lull descended. It was now 10 o'clock; the situation was still one of stalemate. Better deadlocked than dead, the defenders still standing could dare to believe that their plight might yet have a successful outcome. The pause in hostilities, however, brought on an awareness of their weariness.

They were exhausted and, worse, dried out, near complete dehydration. If they were running out of water, they were running out of ammunition also. They were exhausted, some shocked by the violence and exposure to raw fear. Their physical and emotional reserves were dipping towards a low ebb, reaching their limits. Their successful resistance to the Zulu hostility, a defiance of death itself, a disobedience to the inevitable almost, had brought on a certain confidence but its flip-side was an awareness of their present fragility and creeping vulnerability. Hope and despair, certainty and doubt, two sides of the same coin, competed together at once on battlefields of their own. The two most overriding feelings, however, were the desire to drink and a suddenly descending weariness. It was now that many became aware of their cuts and bruises, but not enough to take their minds of their overwhelming thirst and tiredness.

A water-cart full of water stood enticingly close by, only twenty-five yards across the 'no man's land' of the compound yard, near the burning hospital building. Its recovery would be a high-risk undertaking, but better to face the possibility of harm than to die of dehydration – some of the sick and wounded were already dangerously close to doing so. Lieutenant Bromhead mounted a dash across the highly exposed compound yard to retrieve the water-cart. With a covering party, rifles at the ready, Private Hook who had helped to evacuate the hospital among them, while two or three others, perhaps including John William Fielding, recovered the water-cart without incident and pushed it back to the retrenchment biscuit-box parade. Bottles were filled from hoses attached to the cart, drunk from, and refilled. The quenching of their thirst was an enormous morale boost. They would be 'right' for a while more after this. But what then? They were weak and strong all at the same time. Was it futile to continue to defend? But then perhaps the Zulus were asking themselves, was it it futile to continue to attack?

They had made it to midnight, but would they see the light of the coming day?

'DAWN CHORUS'

The lull that descended after the break in fighting was a psychological ordeal for the defenders. A restless edginess ran throughout the post, each one contending with his own fear, uncertain and apprehensive about when the next Zulu attack would begin. The night silence was broken intermittently by nervous exchanges of gunfire or the Zulu *izinduna* shouting out commands in the darkness. Were they mustering for another onslaught? Was all this apparent inactivity by the Zulus a deception, and were they in fact adopting new tactics by changing from an all-out assault to an attempt at infiltration?

The early hours of the morning saw the flames from the burning hospital building begin to fade. Embers continued to fall down, sparks flew about and fiery particles rose in the air. Chard described the situation at this point,

> About midnight or a little after, the fire slackened and after that, although they kept us constantly on the alert, by feigning as before, to come on at different points, the fire was of a desultory character. Our men were careful, and only fired when they could see a fair chance. The flame of the burning hospital was now getting low and as pieces of the roof fell,

Surgeon Major Henry Reynolds giving medical attention to a wounded soldier.

(Illustration by Ray Fitzpatrick)

or hitherto unburnt parts of the thatch ignited, the flames would blaze up, illuminating our helmets and faced – a few shots from the Zulus, replied to by our men – again silence, broken by the same thing repeatedly happening. This sort of thing went on until about 4.00 am and we were anxiously waiting for daybreak and the renewal of the attack, which their comparative and at length complete silence led us to expect . . .

Surgeon Reynolds continued throughout the night to convey constant care and attention to the wounded and sick. There were at least ten badly wounded, two of them critical. He had to remain observant and give consideration to those within the perimeter, although there was much else to concentrate his mind in relation to what lay without. He most likely discussed their shared predicament with James Dalton, down with a wounded shoulder, and passed words of encouragement to Walter Dunne, as well as heartening Chard and Bromhead in their command. They both, along with the rest of the defenders, gazed fixedly and nervously out into the darkness to detect any early signs of a gathering mass of Zulus assembling for a charge, or being marshalled for a combined attack on all sides at once. The tension was exacerbated when the war-cry 'Usuthu, Usuthu, Usuthu' was chanted, only to be heard again shortly afterwards from a different direction in a feigned attack to keep the defenders guessing as to their intentions.

Neither side had in fact the whip hand, yet each thought the other did. The Zulus had come to Rorke's Drift to 'wash their spears in the blood of the red soldiers'. They had attacked the post's perimeter for hours but had been unable to effect a break-in. Now they appeared to have paused. At the same time the defenders realised they themselves were losing their capacity to defend against a further series of attacks. They were exhausted and the strain of defending against the arduous attacks for hours had taken its toll, physically and mentally. The grim reality of their situation was beginning to sink in even more. They feared the dark and what might be concealed in it, but they dreaded the dawn and what would surely come with it. In any 'tight' situation, of which this was an extreme instance, soldiers share a certain fatalism, having known in their hearts on the day they 'donned the uniform' that a situation such as this would arrive and was probably inescapable. They would fight come the light of dawn and stay fighting and sell their lives dearly until their moment came, when force of numbers would ultimately win out and courage would not be enough to forestall the inevitable.

Then they heard it, their thoughts interrupted by the unmistakeable bitter-sweet notes filling each man with a dark foreboding. The 'dawn chorus' had arrived, and shortly after must come the Zulus.

CULMINATION

The first rays of dawn on 23 January 1879 were accompanied by a sense among the defenders that they were about to enter the climax of the battle, that the brightening sky in the east was not only ushering in a new day but also an inevitable end to their lives. But little did they realise, that the climax had already been reached and was over: the Zulus had gone!

Under cover of darkness the Zulu regiments had withdrawn, leaving behind a rearguard which subsequently also slipped away undetected. The Zulus had been where they should not have been, doing what they should not have been doing, and could not make the progress they thought they should. Prince Dabulamanzi had overreached. Now there were many Zulus dead in heaps strewn about the barricades, many more wounded would not live, and many who survived would have to endure horrible, life-long afflictions. The 'red soldiers' had kept fighting longer than the Zulus thought they would, and it appeared that they would continue to do so. The defenders had brought the Zulu attacks to a standstill. The fighting had reached its culmination and was now over. The significance of what had happened was at first hard to take in. If it was difficult twelve hours before to believe the Zulus were arriving, it was more difficult now to believe they had departed. Surgeon Reynolds described the situation,

> *During the whole night following, desultory firing was carried on by the*
> *enemy, and several feigned attacks were made, but nothing of a continued*
> *or determined effort was again attempted by them. About six o'clock*
> *a.m., we found, after careful reconnoitring, that all the Zulus with the*
> *exception of a couple of stragglers had left our immediate vicinity, and*
> *soon afterwards a large body of men were seen at a distance marching*
> *towards us. I did not think it possible that men could have behaved better*
> *than did the 2/24th and the Army Hospital Corps who were particularly*
> *forward during the whole attack.*

Not all the Zulus were gone, as the dead and the dying remained, and in the grey half light of dawn their sprawled bodies lay distorted in ugly, twisted piles around the barricades, monuments to mankind's insane and incomprehensible impulse for war-making.

Could the new light reveal, however, new surprises to confound the defenders' already dazed disbelief? Could they yet be caught unawares by something unforeseen? Could they be caught off guard by the return of the Zulus? This realisation jolted them from their euphoric state, once again bringing them back to harsh reality. The more they thought about it, the possibility of a new Zulu attack remained real.

Conscious of their continuing vulnerability, they realised it was again time to anticipate and prepare. Work-parties were detailed to drag the Zulu corpses clear of the mealie-bags, and these barricades were repaired and improved. Work began to clear the fields of fire in the shrubbery area in front of the hospital building, which had proved so problematic. Zulu weapons were gathered, and the burned-out remains of the hospital was attended to so that it might not provide cover for the Zulus. The roof of the storehouse had to be de-thatched so it could not be set on fire. Any and all perceived advantages that could benefit the Zulus were dealt with. Finally, a grim but practical contingency was taken care of in the establishment of a temporary mortuary. This involved a number of upsetting elements and was a horrific aspect to the aftermath of battle. The discovery of Private Garret Hayden's severely disfigured body, with its many mutilations, struck a particularly deep and sombre note among the tiny garrison. No less harrowing was the removal of Sergeant Maxwell's badly charred body from the hospital building. They were covered and laid out side by side with their dead colleagues in the cattle-kraal and a sentry posted to prevent needless attention being paid to them and granting them a respect in repose.

One pleasant surprise came with the return of those who had broken out of the hospital building during its attack. Gunner Howard and Private Waters re-joined the garrison, having laid out under the cover of darkness undetected by the Zulus. A third escapee, Private Beckett, was discovered by a patrol, near death but still alive, and was brought to Surgeon Reynolds' attention, but unfortunately he was to succumb subsequently to his injuries.

There were fifteen fallen already accounted for, including Corporal Anderson (NNC), shot immediately before the beginning of the battle by the post's defenders. Later, Private Beckett and a fatally wounded Lance-Sergeant Williams were to join this total, giving an astonishingly small number of seventeen dead defenders, most of them having died as a result of gunshot wounds rather than spear thrusts. There were eight seriously wounded; many more had minor cuts and wounds.

The victors' worst fears, however, became dramatically realised, and they had quickly to become defenders again. The Zulus were back!

The alarming sight of a large body of Zulus moving back into position on the forward slope of KwaSingquindi hill near Shiyane hill made the garrison immediately abandon their tasks, withdraw inside the perimeter, and adopt all-round defence 'stand-to' positions in preparation for further fighting. They waited for the Zulus to make the next move.

The Zulus were curiously slow to initiate a re-engagement. A strange stand-off developed, as the Zulus, instead of sweeping forward as usual, continued to watch the 'red soldiers' down below them. The defenders once again put bullets into the breech chambers of their Martini-Henry rifles, released the cocking mechanisms, and waited for the heat of battle to recommence. All this was done in the dazed detachment that accompanies exhaustion and exposure to extreme danger. They stood watching, waiting, wondering about their prospects of surviving another attack. Having endured so much for so long against huge odds, it was hardly credible to expect that they could continue to outlive a further series of assaults.

Such thoughts were interrupted by a sudden movement – not a movement from the forward slope of KwaSingquindi hill, but by horsemen cantering up towards them from the Drift. These were the forward elements of Lieutenant-General Lord Chelmsford's column. These were their salvation. These meant the defence of Rorke's Drift was delivered, and with it their lives.

Lieutenant-Colonel John Russell and Lieutenant Henry Walsh of the Imperial Mounted Infantry rode in at the head of their detachment, accompanied by Captain Penn Symons of the 24th, and Charles 'Noggs' Norris-Newman, a newspaper correspondent.

Assistant Commissary Walter Dunne remembered the moment as follows,

> *Approaching cautiously at first, a mounted officer, when reassured, galloped up and anxiously enquired if any of the men from Isandlwana had escaped*

and joined us. Sadly we answered, 'No'. Overcome by the emotion at the terrible certainty conveyed by that short word, he bent down to his horse's neck trying in vain to stifle the sobs from his overcharged heart. No wonder his grief mastered him for he had passed during the night by that camp where hundreds of his brave comrades lay slaughtered, and the hope that some portion may have fought their way through was crushed forever.

The defenders were now fully aware of what they had been spared. The column's arrival had ensured their safety and, unlike their seventeen fallen comrades and the hundreds at Isandlwana, they would continue to live. In defending the outpost against a vastly superior force of courageous and determined Zulu warriors, the tiny garrison had fought with a gritty resilience for their lives, and survived.

The Return of the Colour *by Lieutenant William Whitelock Lloyd, published in the* Illustrated London News, *29 March 1879.*

AFTERMATH

A Zulu voice today, that of Mphiwa Ntanza, relates the description of what happened at Rorke's Drift handed down by his great-grandfather Lusizi, a Zulu warrior of the uDloko,

> *We attacked Rorke's Drift so that we could 'wash our spears', many so that they could at last marry. For many it was their first time to fight and it was very hard because at Rorke's Drift there was the 'laager' [fortified post] and we could not apply the 'horns of the beast', and the defenders kept up a constant firing . . . 'bang bang . . . bang bang . . . bang bang', ..they kept firing and kept firing . On return, because we had disobeyed the chief's order not to cross the Buffalo River, we were each fined five cattle.*

The Rorke's Drift post defenders had extricated themselves from an extreme entanglement and an acute difficulty. They had survived when the odds were heavily stacked against them, they had thwarted the most likely outcome by their courage and defiance. By any standards they had experienced an extraordinarily exceptional event, bringing it to an improbable conclusion, and their soldiery efforts deserved huge appreciation and admiration. They did not exude exuberance outwardly; rather it was a repressed ebullience befitting the soldiers of the Victorian era.

The defenders had a range of reactions to their dramatic participation, manifesting in behaviours as individual and different as the personalities involved. Private Michael Minehan found himself unable to speak for a time after the event, communicating his skewering of the Zulu by the cattle-kraal's inner stone wall by gesture alone. Acting Assistant Commissary James Dalton, caught up in the defence's very inception and its fulsome execution, was the very next day, despite having received a serious wound, handing out food to the troops as normal. Others, perhaps all, were haunted or troubled to lesser or greater degrees by harrowing memories of their ordeal. The mental trauma, the emotional shock following the stressful episode, was to play out in their minds in the short and long terms in different ways.

Chelmsford's column on arrival allowed the post's defenders to stand down and rest in the attic space of the storehouse. They then set about burying the dead, tended to the wounded and further fortified the post, stone walls replacing the mealie-bag barricades. The Zulu wounded left dying on the battlefield around the post were ruthlessly killed outright. No mercy was shown them as the column members knew that no compassion had been received by their colleagues at Isandlwana. This was war, in which an absence of humanity, a barbarous heartlessness, pervaded. There were 351 bodies put into graves on the day following. Many more Zulu dead were subsequently discovered; a full and accurate total tally was never actually recorded.

Neither was there to be an end to their own dead. The lack of shelter from the incessant nightly downpours, their canvas covers having been destroyed in both battles, meant there was little protection from the elements. Over the coming weeks, the sodden and cramped conditions proved rife breeding ground for the spread of typhoid and dysentery, some succumbing to these sicknesses and otherwise to the squalid misery, the filth, and the quagmire.

The lost Queen's Colour of the 1st/24th was sought, a search aided by the now receding water levels of early February. The Colour's retrieval before their departure would restore some measure of regimental morale in the face of such huge losses at Isandlwana. Colonel Richard Glyn, since the early departure of Chelmsford to Pietermaritzburg on 24 January, was in charge, and he had the post and fortifications built up, and instilled a strict awareness of security.

Notwithstanding the perceived security risks, Glyn sanctioned the searching of the banks of the Buffalo River downstream at Sothondose's Drift. In preparation for this undertaking, on the evening beforehand, a small mounted party from the Natal Native Contingent irregulars was sent out to reconnoitre the vicinity of the intended search area. It was not long before they made the dramatic discovery of the clearly recognisable bodies of Lieutenants Nevill Coghill and Teignmouth Melvill. Placing stones over the bodies, they returned to Rorke's Drift. An early start by the main search party the next morning was not long in making the remarkable find of the precious silk Colour itself, the pole of which was sticking straight up out of the water near mid-river. Retrieved with great joy, it was carried jubilantly back to Rorke's Drift. It had first been formerly presented to the regiment when they were stationed at the Curragh Camp, Co. Kildare, in 1866, some thirteen years beforehand; poignantly, very few who were present then remained alive to see its return, having been cruelly slain at Isandlwana.

The retrieval of the Queen's Colour was good news for the regiment and for the army. But the wider circumstance in which it had been lost was not. The news about Isandlwana was received in Britain as a total shock, one of the worst defeats of a British force in the Victorian era to date. It was all the more regarded as a complete catastrophe because part of a modern professional army with state-of-the-art weaponry had been defeated by what were regarded as primitive natives armed only with spears, shields and clubs. Worse than failure, it was seen as an incomprehensible fiasco. There was some huge measure of comfort taken then when the initial reports of the subsequent happenings at Rorke's Drift began to filter through. Further newspaper articles with fuller accounts and more detail communicated the news of an unlikely victory against impossible odds, thus restoring pride in the 'pluck' of the British soldier and the rebalancing of faith in the British military. The defence of Rorke's Drift was heralded as the epitome of successful soldering, and was celebrated both as a contrast to Isandlwana and in its own right. If a defeat ever needed an immediate victory to follow it, than Isandlwana certainly required one. That a victory at Rorke's Drift was forthcoming, particularly in such circumstances was astonishing. The tiny Rorke's Drift garrison had performed exceptionally, the Irish among them no less so.

But what now? Colonel Glyn and what was left of the main column (No. 3) were on the Natal side of the border at Rorke's Drift awaiting further orders, while Colonel Evelyn Wood and No. 4 Column were in the north, and Colonel Charles Pearson and No. 1 Column were on the coast near Eshowe, both columns still inside Zululand, hunkered down and adopting a more defensive posture as they did not want their commands to share a similar fate to Isandlwana. The offensive invasion was immobilised, Pearson's column harassed by Prince Dabulamangi and Wood's by Prince Mbilini. Fears of a Zulu counter-invasion into Natal caused a degree of hysteria, and many throughout the colony began to busy themselves with building barricades and reinforcing settlements. It was not, and never had been, Cetshwayo's intent to undertake such a venture, and all the while he was holding out for a negotiated settlement with the British. This defensive strategy, however, handed the initiative back to the British, with ultimately fatal results for his kingdom. Some at home were not happy with the British colonists in Natal. In fact, the Prime Minister Benjamin Disraeli was intensely disapproving of Frere's and Chelmsford's actions. Chelmsford, however, benefitted from support by the Queen and, for the present, the more benign attitude of the Commander-in-Chief, HRH the Duke of Cambridge. The War Office despatched reinforcements to South Africa, six infantry battalions, two batteries of artillery, and two regiments of cavalry; the crushing defeat at Isandlwana could not go unanswered. There was now a determination to wage a war and to win it. It would take time for the reinforcements to arrive and for the time being various actions at Ntombi Drift, Hlobane and Kambula occupied Colonel Wood's command, while Chelmsford, learning the lessons from Isandlwana, moved 5,000 troops across the Tugela river to successfully extricate Pearson's force from Eshowe, but not before having to confront a Zulu force over twice that of his own at Gingindlovu. On this occasion, having remained consciously concentrated in a measured and deliberate advance, each evening forming his wagons into a great square, he dug defence trenches around them. The confrontation when it came saw a number of brave frontal Zulu assaults wilt under the weight of the intense defence of the British force from such a prepared position. Chelmsford then, along with Pearson's rescued force, withdrew to Natal to wait the reinforcements from Britain. On their arrival (11 April 1879) the various units combined to reconstitute a second invasion force which launched itself back into Zululand on 31 May 1879. Pressing ahead with the advance, they eventually arrived at Cetshwayo's capital, Ulundi, and forming an enormous moving square (with over thirty infantry companies, ten artillery pieces and two Gatling guns in the centre, and the cavalry) they moved against the Zulu force and within an hour the Anglo-Zulu War was over. Cetshwayo himself was eventually captured fifty-five days later and subsequently sent into exile. Lieutenant General Sir Garrett Wolseley had arrived and took over Chelmsford's command twelve days after the Ulundi battle. Chelmsford returned to Britain a victor, believing himself devoid of any culpability for what happened at Isandlwana. In early May the *London Gazette* contained the news that Chard, Bromhead, Allen, Hitch, Hook, John William (Fielding), and the two Jones, Robert and Fielding, had been awarded the Victoria Cross, the highest number ever to a single unit for a single action. There was no mention of Dalton, Dunne, or Surgeon Reynolds!

General Sir Garrett Wolseley partitioned Zululand into thirteen separate regions, each ruled by 'a kinglet' who had some loyalty to the British. This proved disastrous and civil war followed. The chaos resulted in the annexation of Zululand as a British colony on 19 May 1887. Unrest followed and the subsequent Usuthu uprising raged until it was finally put to an end in August 1888.

The Mission Station at Rorke's Drift.
(Courtesy of the Regimental Museum of the Royal Welsh, Brecon, Wales)

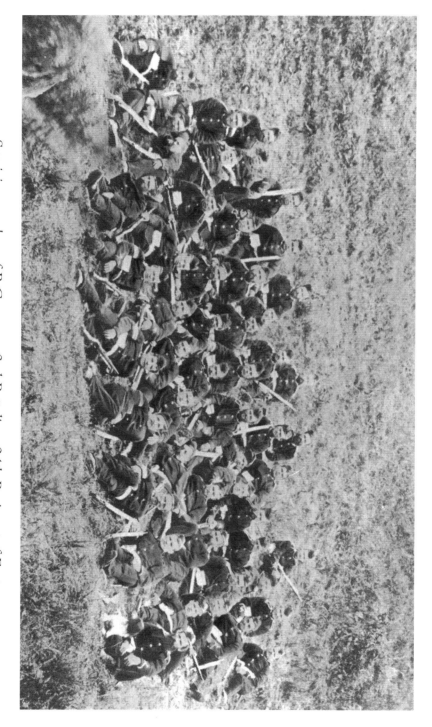

Surviving members of B Company, 2nd Battalion, 24th Regiment of Foot.
(Courtesy of the Regimental Museum of the Royal Welsh, Brecon, Wales)

LIFE AFTER RORKE'S DRIFT

While Chelmsford's military career appeared to progress by the awarding of a series of outwardly appealing appointments, this advancement was more apparent than real. With the passage of time and fuller information, the military establishment came to hold him alone responsible for the chronic conduct of the early part of the Zulu war campaign leading to the ignominious failure of Isandlwana.

It took time also for Acting Assistant Commissary James Dalton's contribution to be recognised. It was largely due to his experience that the defence at Rorke's Drift was a success. At first his participation was not acknowledged, but reports of his involvement and actions, having reached the notice of senior officers and even Queen Victoria herself, he was eventually awarded his VC by General Hugh Clifford VC at a special parade at Fort Napier on 16 January 1880. He returned to army service, being given a permanent commission as a commissary officer (the equivalent of a first lieutenant). He sailed for England in February and the London *Evening Standard* of St Patrick's Day 1880 reported: 'Assistant Commissary James Langley Dalton VC arrived at the [Windsor] Castle to-day, and had the honour of an interview with the Queen.' He returned to South Africa as a civilian gold prospector in the Transvaal but did not make his fortune and moved instead to his more familiar surroundings in the Eastern Cape. Eight years after his courageous conduct at Rorke's Drift, Dalton died of natural causes on 7 January 1887 in a Port Elizabeth Hotel. He had never married and was buried in the Russell Road Roman Catholic Cemetery.

Lieutenant Gonville ('Gunny') Bromhead, like Lieutenant John Chard, received an immediate brevet to major. Lieutenant-General Sir Garrett Wolsey presented him with his VC at Utrecht on 22 August 1879. He had been invited to Balmoral to see the Queen at the same time as Chard, but as circumstances worked out he was in Ireland, fishing. He was to continue in service and soldiered in Gibraltar, India, and in the Burma Campaign of 1886-88. He remained a single man and at the age of 46, having returned to India he fell ill with fever and died at Camp Dabhaura, Allahabad on 8 February 1891, twelve years after Rorke's Drift.

Private John William Fielding, son of Michael Fielding and Margaret Godsil, both of Cork City, after his heroic exploits aiding the escapees from the hospital building at Rorke's Drift, continued to soldier with the 2nd/24th for a duration, and it was while in Gibraltar that he was presented with his Victoria Cross by Major General Anderson. From Gibraltar he went to India and then discharge in 1883. He took up employment in a civilian post at Brecon Barracks and married an Irish girl, Elizabeth Murphy, with whom he had five children. He re-enlisted during his fifties for the duration of the Great War in the role of recruiting sergeant. Private John William Fielding was to go on and be the longest surviving Rorke's Drift VC winner, dying of natural causes at the age of 75 on 23 November 1932. He was to outlive his wife Elizabeth, and so too sadly his eldest son Tom who was killed on the Western Front during the Great War on the retreat from Mons. John Fielding VC was buried on 29 November 1932 in St. Michael's, Llantarnam, Monmouthshire.

Surgeon James Henry Reynolds received immediate promotion to surgeon-major but was not among those initially nominated for the VC. He remained on active service in South Africa and was present at the Battle of Ulundi on 4 July 1879, witnessing the final defeat of the Zulu army. His distinguished service at Rorke's Drift finally appreciated, he was presented with his VC by Colonel Richard Glyn at Pinetown on 26 August 1879. A year after Rorke's Drift he was back in Dublin and stationed at Richmond Barracks and was treated as a hero on his return. Trinity College, Dublin, awarded him an honorary doctorate, the Royal College of Physicians of Ireland made him a fellow, and the British Medical Association awarded him their Gold Medal. He married Elizabeth Mary McCormack of Westbrook, Glenealy, Co. Wicklow, and they were to have four children. Shortly after his wedding he was transferred to the Mayo-Sligo area in late 1880 with the 19th Royal Hussars during the operation to relieve Captain Charles Boycott during the Irish Land War. Their first child, George, was born in Co. Sligo in 1882, and the following three, Percival (1884), Harry (1885), and Lilly (1886) in Dublin. As a result of the birth of Lilly or complications afterwards, Elizabeth died aged 30 on 8 December 1886 and was was buried in Glasnevin Cemetery. James Henry Reynolds never remarried. Transferred to England, he was promoted Lieutenant-Colonel on 1 April 1887 and retired two years later in January 1896. Made medical administrator of the Royal Army Clothing Factory in Pimlico, he had an active retirement, travelling frequently. He died in 1932 and was buried in St Mary's Catholic Cemetery, Kensal Green, London.

The lesser known logistician at Rorke's Drift was Corkman Walter Adolphus Dunne. His heroic labours and formidable courage atop the mealie-bag mount, moulding it into a redoubt while exposed to Zulu gunfire and spears, did not earn him a VC despite his being nominated for it, but it did earn him huge reputational respect. Born on 10 February

1853, he was baptised in the South Parish Church (Civil Parish of St Nicholas). His father was the secretary of the Country Club, 80 South Mall, which would have been a well-paid position. The family moved to Dublin when his father became manager at the St Stephen's Green Club. When Walter wanted to join the army in 1872 he had to get an affirmation as regards his age. James Dunne signed it on 24 August 1872 and it was verified by Thomas Butler, Justice of the Peace, Co. Tipperary, who most likely was staying in the St Stephen's Green Club at the time. This was probably done because a birth certificate was required but these were not introduced in Ireland until 1864.

The Morning Post of 5 May 1875 announced that Walter Alphonsus Dunne had been promoted from sub-assistant commissary to assistant commissary in the Supply and Transport Department. Dunne had seen previous extensive active service against the Xhosa. After Rorke's Drift he continued to serve throughout the Zulu War and then against the Boers in the 1881 Transvaal Rebellion, taking part in the defence of Potchesfstroom. He was to serve in the Egyptian War of 1882 and was present at the battle of Tel-el-Kebir and in the Sudan campaign in 1885. He was promoted to lieutenant-colonel in 1888, made CB (Companion of the Bath) in 1896, and promoted colonel in 1896. He married Winifred Bind, daughter of John Bind, CMG, the Treasurer of Natal on 23 July 1885, and a daughter was born in 1887. Walter Dunne retired from service in February 1908 after thirty-five years, during which he had seen a number of wars close up. Moving to Gibraltar in February 1908, possibly for health reasons, he died a few months later on 2 July 1908 in the English Nursing Home in Rome. Lieutenant John Chard had made strong testimony as to Dunne's 'much exposed' courageous actions building the redoubt at Rorke's Drift, but despite this and the muted support of Chelmsford, the matter was finally decided by HRH the Duke of Cambridge, Commander-in-Chief, who on 18 October 1879 declared, 'We are giving the VC very freely I think, but probably

Mr Dalton had as good a claim as the others who have got the Cross for Rorke's Drift Defence. I don't think there is a case for Mr Dunne.'

'The Quiet Sergeant', Henry Gallagher, from Thurles, Co. Tipperary, initially among those on the south (rear) wall, later atop the mealie-bag redoubt, had a life-long reminder of the battle in the blue/black tattooing effect on the side of his right check and nose, which had resulted from a burning flash back from the over-heated chamber breech of his Martini-Henry rifle. Moved to Utrecht, he took no further part in the Zulu War and returned to home service, spending at first almost ten months in Gibraltar, and was promoted to colour-sergeant in January 1881. With his wife Caroline, he had six children, the second of whom, Henry Edward, was later to join the Royal Engineers, while the third, William Alfred, also served with them, later transferring to the Royal Signals as a major, while yet another son, Lawrence Stanley, also served in the Royal Engineers but completed his army career as a colonel with the Royal Artillery. Henry himself was to receive further promotions and was eventually made garrison sergeant-major in Cairo, the last of his many further overseas postings which included India, Burma and Aden, in a career lasting twenty-three years, retiring on 10 May 1897. He immediately took up an appointment as barrack warden at Coleworth Barracks, Hilsea, and Alexandria Hospital until 1911. He died at the age of 75 on 17 December 1931.

Corporal James Bushe (St John's Parish, Dublin), wounded in the nose by a bullet that had killed Private Cole, was appointed lance-corporal shortly after Rorke's Drift. He left South Africa early the following year to serve in India. He was to serve in Burma and again in India before returning to Britain and his discharge in October 1891.

Private Michael Minehan, whom shock and exhaustion had temporarily rendered unable to talk following his experiences at the defence of Rorke's Drift, was to serve in India, where he had done so before South

Africa. He was discharged from the army in September 1884 as a result of cholera contacted there. Lieutenant Gonville Bromhead wrote him a testimonial on discharge.

Many of the participants of the famous defence of Rorke's Drift went on to lead interesting, full and rewarding lives, men like Patrick Gagley born in St Patrick's Parish in Cork City who had joined the 24th Regiment of Foot in Cork on 10 March 1865 as a boy soldier. From a family with a military background (there are 'Patrick Gagleys' from Cork City joining regiments from the 1820s to the First World War) this Patrick Gagley was a regimental drummer with the 24th. After Rorke's Drift he left the army in March 1880 and married a Welsh lady named Catherine, eleven years his senior. They had no children. Patrick lived a long life, dying at the age of 84 in London on 11 August 1935. He is buried in Paddington Old Cemetery. So too with another Cork-born participant, Private John Manley, who survived the battle and on returning from the war became a house painter and married Ellen Carroll, with whom he had six children.

For all of these Rorke's Drift veterans whose later lives were made up of decades of everyday normality, as well as those whose reality may have been less fortunate, the battle's yearly anniversary was unlikely to pass without bringing back recollections of those fateful twelve hours, some perhaps never fully recovered from the harrowing experience to once again become unsettled, and maybe morose, gloomy and unsociable, others reflecting on a prized, dearly held private pride, remembering the satisfaction of a challenge faced, of courage found, and of a camaraderie forged in the furnace of battle. Chance and circumstance had placed them at the epicentre of an extraordinary event. They were dramatically enveloped in an exciting and extreme episode, the sudden supreme defence of their post when attacked by overwhelming numbers of Zulu warriors in a savage and sustained onslaught. Their reaction became the epitome of soldierly example, the essence of which was an unequivocal fighting spirit. They were ordinary soldiers who in extraordinary circumstances displayed a resolve that still astonishes. It remains a truly remarkable story whose future recounting must now necessarily include the inspirational input of Acting Assistant Commissary James Langley Dalton, the many incredible incidences of bravery by Surgeon James Henry Reynolds, Private John William Fielding, Acting Commissary Walter Adolphus Dunne, and Lieutenant Gonville Bromhead; and finally the courageous involvement of an overall significant Irish presence, all central to this spectacular story.

After the battle, the Mission Station at Rorke's Drift (looking north).
(Courtesy of the Regimental Museum of the Royal Welsh, Brecon, Wales)

In 1898 a gathering of holders of the Victoria Cross was photographed at the unveiling of the Anglo-Zulu War Memorial Plaque in Brecon, Wales. Their names are as follows:
Back row, from left, Pte Robert Jones VC, Pte Alfred Hook VC, Pte William Jones VC.
Front row, from left, Pte David Bell VC, Col E S Brown VC, Pte Fred Hitch VC, Pte John Fielding VC.
(Courtesy of the Regimental Museum of the Royal Welsh, Brecon, Wales)

1. Pte Robert Jones VC, won Cross at Rorke's Drift. Born 19 August 1857 at Tynewydd Nr Raglan; committed suicide (disputed, may have been shooting accident) 6 Sept 1898; buried in St Peter's Churchyard, Peterchurch. At time of burial coffin taken over church wall rather than through gate, headstone facing opposite to all others in churchyard due to Jones's alleged suicide.

2. Pte Alfred Hook VC, won Cross at Rorke's Drift. Born 6 August 1850 at Birdwood, Churcham, Glocs, died 12 March 1905 of consumption, buried in Churcham, St Andrew's parish church. Worked in British Museum as an inside duster, later promoted to umbrella attendant.

3. Pte William Jones VC, won Cross at Rorke's Drift. Born 16 August 1839 in Bristol, died 15 April 1913, buried in Phillips Park Cemetery, Manchester. Pawned VC for £5 to feed his family then later sold pawn ticket. Just before death was found wandering the streets of Manchester under the illusion the Zulus were coming to get him. Note that he is not wearing his VC in the photo, due to the medal having been pawned.

4. Pte David Bell VC, won Cross at Little Andaman Islands, 7 May 1867 saving men from island inhabited by cannibals. Born 1845 Co Down died 7 March 1920, buried Woodlands Cemetery, Gillingham. [Pte William Griffith VC, not shown in this group, won his VC in the same incident, later killed 22 Jan 1879 at Isandlwana.

5. Col Browne won Cross at Inhlobana, 29 March 1879 rescuing stranded Mounted infantrymen. Born 23 Dec 1852, Cambridge, died 16 July 1907, buried Clarens Cemetery, Chemin de Munraz, Montreaux.

6. Pte Frederick Hitch VC, won Cross at Rorke's Drift. Born 29 Nov 1856 Southgate, Middlesex, died 6 Jan 1913 of pneumonia and heart failure due to picket duty while on strike as a cabby after the Home Secretary (Winston Churchill) increased the price of petrol but did not allow fares to be increased at the time; Hitch is buried in Chiswick cemetery.

7. Pte John Fielding VC (aka John Williams), won Cross at Rorke's Drift; joined the army as John Williams to avoid his father knowing of enlistment; born 24 May 1857 in Abergavenny, died 25th Nov 1932, buried Llantaman, Monmouthshire.

APPENDICES

CHRONOLOGY

1300	Far-off firing form Isandlwana begins to be heard at Rorke's Drift; it does not arouse urgency or any sense of grave danger
1515	Survivors from Isandlwana begin to arrive at Rorke's Drift; precariousness of situation is now appreciated.
1630	Advance party of Zulu appears; initial assault on Rorke's Drift.
1650	Main party of Zulus arrives, takes up position in front of hospital with riflemen placed at Shiyane hill rock terrace; several severe attacks on hospital area, battle begins in earnest.
1830	Post garrison falls back behind biscuit-box barricade due to heavy incoming fire from Shiyane rock terrace but mostly because of seriousness of heavy assaults at barricade in front of storehouse.

1900	Darkness descends; hospital set on fire and abandoned.
1930	Defence against ongoing attacks aided by light from burning hospital building.
2000	Zulu main point of attack switches to eastern end of the post, permeating through cattle kraal but is checked.
2100	Attacks ongoing
2200	Zulu assaults losing impetus but fire fight continues throughout night.
0400 hours	Last recorded shots by Zulus
0430	Dawn – Zulu have withdrawn but garrison makes ready for another assault.
0700	Zulus appear, then retire
0800	Lord Chelmsford's column arrives

THE IRISH AT ISANDLWANA

There were numerous Irish in the 1st Battalion, 24th Regiment of Foot, who died at Isandlwana. The 1st/24th had well above the average norm of twenty-two percent of Irish members for the time. Irish names included Bennett, Collins, Connolly, Donohue, Kelly, Mahony, Murphy, Burke, Fitzgerald, Harrington, Holland, Egan, and Walsh, and while one can access their service numbers, unfortunately their service records, which would have confirmed where they came from and, with some additional work, reveal details of their families, have not survived. Service records were kept for pension purposes, but unfortunately none of these survived to collect their pensions. Mention has already been made of Lieutenant Nevill Coghill, who was heroically involved in trying to save the battalion's Queen Colour, and who had a strong family connection with Castletownshend, Co. Cork. Also we have become familiar with the participation of Colonel Anthony Durnford, born in Manorhamilton, Co. Leitrim. It was he who was the subject of Lord Chelmsford's insinuations when he attempted to make him a scapegoat for the defeat, when it is now clear that it was Chelmsford himself who was responsible for the many lives lost – amongst whom was an Irish holder of the Victoria Cross, Private William Griffiths, born in 1841 in Co. Roscommon. On 7 May 1867, at the island of Little Andaman, in the Bay of Bengal, Private Griffiths was one of a party of five (David Bell, James Cooper, Campbell Mellis Douglas, and Thomas Murphy) of the 2nd/24th who risked their lives in manning a boat and proceeding though dangerous surf to rescue some of their comrades who had been sent to the island to find out the fate of the commander and seven crew members who had landed from the *Assam Valley* and were feared murdered by the cannibalistic islanders. At Isandlwana, he and many others were annihilated, having been left utterly exposed and vulnerable because of Chelmsford's deeply held but erroneous conviction that the Zulus would never dare to attack in open battle against the well-known firepower of a modern army.

THE IRISH AT RORKE'S DRIFT

The cumulative presence of Irishmen at Rorke's Drift, including native Irish-born, others born of Irish parents in Britain, and those with Irish names and connections suggests this 'Irish' participation to have consisted of the following;

Native Irish-born:

Surgeon James Henry Reynolds VC, Dublin;
Assistant Commissary Walter Dunne, South Parish Cork;

Sergeant Henry Gallagher, Thurles Co. Tipperary;

Privates James Bush, St John's, Dublin;

Timothy Connors. Killeaty, Co. Cork;

James Dick, Islandmagee, Co. Antrim;

James Hagan, Nenagh, Co. Tipperary;

Thomas Lynch, Limerick;

Michael Minehan, Castlehaven, Co. Cork;

Augustus Morris, Dublin;

Thomas Robinson, St. Patrick's, Dublin;

Michael Tobin, Windygap, Co. Kilkenny;

Drummer Patrick Hayes, Newmarket, Co. Clare;

Private Henry Turner, Ballsbridge, Dublin;

Drummer Patrick Galgey, St Patrick's, Cork;

Private John Manley, Cork;

Private Garret Hayden, Dublin;

Private Michael Kiley, Mitchelstown, Co. Cork.

Born of Irish parents in Britain or elsewhere:

Lieutenant Gonville 'Gunny' Bromhead VC, born in France, parents Edmund (50% Irish) and Judith Wood (100% Irish);

Acting Assistant Commissary James Langley Dalton VC, born in London, parents most likely from the Westmeath-Longford area;

Private John William Fielding VC, born in Abergavenny, Monmouthshire, Wales, of Cork City parents Michael Fielding and Margaret Godsil;

Corporal John 'Jack' Jeremiah Lyons, born in Pontypool, Monmouthshire, Wales, of Cork parents John and Mary Lyons

Irish names and connections:

Privates Thomas Buckley;

Anthony Connors;

John Fagan;

John Murphy;

Patrick Desmond;

William Horrigan;

Storeman Louis Byrne;

Private Michael McMahon, Army Hospital Corps.

NOTE: The List includes four VC Winners (Private John Fielding, Lieutenant Gonville Bromhead, Acting Assistant Commissary James Langley Dalton, and Surgeon James Henry Reynolds). Also, Private Michael McMahon was awarded the Distinguished Conduct Medal (DCM) but this award was cancelled by the commander-in-chief in January 1880 because of a charge of absence and theft.

THE IRISH DEAD AT RORKE'S DRIFT

John Fagan;

Patrick Hayden;

William Herrigan;

Louis Byrne.

FAMILY TREE, LIEUTENANT GONVILLE BROMHEAD

GONVILLE BROMHEAD (1845 – 1891)

Born in France

Mother: Judith Christine Wood (1804 – 1876) Woodville Sligo

Father: Edmund Bromhead (1791 – 1870)

Maternal Grandparents

James Wood (Sligo) and Judith Coristine (Sligo)

Paternal Grandparents

Gonville Bromhead and Jane Ffrench (Galway)

NOTE: Lieutenant Gonville 'Gunny' Bromhead's father was half Irish, his mother Irish. Three of his four grandparents were Irish. He was born in France. Being 75% Irish would qualify a person as Irish.

LETTER WRITTEN BY WALTER DUNNE AT RORKE'S DRIFT

Walter Dunne wrote this letter on a chit for bags of mealie to his friend Granville Warneford, son of the resident magistrate, Cape Colony, describing the battle that had been fought at Rorke's Drift the day before:

> *Rorke's Drift, 24 Jan '79*
> *My Dear Warneford,*
> *Sad news about the 1/24th, 5 Cd [companies] commanded bt Col.*
> *Pulleine were cut to pieces and the camp sacked. 20 officers are missing.*
> *About 1000 of the Kafirs came in here and attacked us on the same*
> *day. We had got about 2 hours' notice and fortified the place with*
> *trap of grain biscuit boxes &c. They came on most determinedly on all*
> *sides. They drove our fellows out of the Hospital, killed the patients*
> *and burned the place. They made several attempts to storm us but the*
> *soldiers (B Co of 24th under Bromhead) kept up such a steady killing*
> *fire that they were driven back each time. We had only 80 men, the*

contingent having bolted before a shot was fired. The fight was kept up all night & in the morning the Kafirs retreated leaving 352 dead bodies. Dalton was wounded in the shoulder and temp clerk Byrne killed & 12 of the men . . . Some of the missing are Pulleine, Col Dunford, Capt Russell, Hodson (killed), Anstey, Daly, Mostyn, Dyer, Griffith, Pope, Austin, Pulleine (2 Mr), Shepherd (S . . . major), Wardell (killed), Younghusband. Degacher, Porteous, Carage Dyson, Atkinson – Coghill is believed to have escaped & also Melvill.

AN IRISH SOLDIER-ARTIST IN ZULULAND

Soldiers going overseas on duty, even to war, often brought with them personal effects. These individual items were usually unique to their make-up and temperament and reflect their interests or hobbies. Two months after the defence of Rorke's Drift, 23-year-old Lieutenant William Whitelocke Lloyd, D Company, 2nd/24th, of Strancally Castle, situated on the Blackwater just south of Villierstown in west Waterford, arrived at the top of Shiyane hill, reached into his kitbag and pulled out his sketchbook and his box of watercolours. From this vantage point and others, he sketched over the ensuing months many panoramas and invaluable close-up images detailing daily life on the Zulu campaign. Realistic, accurate, often humorous, sometimes poignant, his art was painted by someone who was there, unlike many of the paintings later synonymous with the Zulu campaign which were created by artists who had never visited South Africa. Lloyd was present during the battle of Ulundi, and aspects of this final encounter which brought an end to the war did not escape his sharp eye. *The Illustrated London News* published a number of his sketches to accompany their reportage of the war. He left the army in 1882, married Catherine Brougham in 1885 and settled in Glandore, Co. Cork, two children, Percy and Winifred, being born to them. He became a professional illustrator with the Peninsula Steamship Company (P&O), drawing pen and ink sketches that were sold to passengers as keepsakes of their voyage. He travelled all over the world and produced three books of sketches depicting life on board these luxury liners and the exotic places through which they passed. In addition, his book *On Active Service* was a collection of mostly humorous sketches of military life. Prior to this, he had never published his Zulu war work and tragically at 41 was killed falling from a tree he was pruning at Glandore in the autumn of 1897. His daughter Winifred held possession of his Zululand album, passing it in 1976 to the Becher family who had cared for her in her old age. Twenty-four years later the Bechers made contact with South African historian David Rattray who put the 150 sketches into a book titled *A Soldier-Artist in Zululand*, with a foreword by Britain's Prince Charles. Rattray himself was tragically shot dead during a break-in at his farm near Rorke's Drift in 2007, not long after the book was published. The Bechers sold the album at Sotheby's on 20 July 2012 for £40,000.

CHARD'S REPORT TO QUEEN VICTORIA

Early in January 1879, shortly after the arrival of the 5th Company, Royal Engineers, at Durban, an order came from Lord Chelmsford directing that an officer and a few good men of the R.E., with mining implements, etc., should join the third column as soon as possible. I was consequently sent on in advance of the company, with a light mule wagon containing the necessary tools etc., and in which the men could also ride on level ground; with a Corporal, three Sappers and one Driver, my batman, who rode one and looked after my horses. The wagon was driven by a Cape black man, with a Natal Kaffir lad as voorlooper. The roads were so bad that in spite of all our exertions, our progress was slow, and although we got a fresh team at Pietermaritzberg, we did not reach Rorke's Drift until the morning of the 19th January 1879. The 3rd Column was encamped on the other side (left bank) of the River Buffalo, and the wagons were still crossing on the ponts. I pitched my two tents on the right (Natal) bank of the river, near the ponts, and close to the store accommodation there for keeping them in repair. On the 20th January, the 3rd Column broke up its camp on the Buffalo River and marched to Isandlwana, where it encamped, and the same evening, or following morning, Colonel Durnford's force arrived and took up its camp near where the 3rd Column had been.

There were two large ponts at the river, one of which only was in working order, and my sappers were during this time working at the other, which was nearly finished, to get it also in working order. Late in the evening of the 21st January I received an order from the 3rd Column to say that the men of the R.E., who had lately arrived were to proceed to the camp at Isandlwana at once. I had received no orders concerning myself. I reported this to Major Spalding, who was now in command at Rorke's Drift, and also pointed out to him that the sappers leaving there was no means at my disposal for putting the ponts in working order, or keeping them so. Major Spalding had also received no orders respecting me, except that I was to select a suitable position protecting the ponts, for Captain Rainsforth's Company 1/24th to entrench itself. I consequently asked and obtained permission from Major Spalding, to go to the camp at Isandlwana and see the orders.

On the morning of the 22nd January, I put the corporal and three sappers in the empty wagon, with their field kits, etc., to take them to the camp of the 3rd Column; and also rode out myself. The road was very heavy in some places, and the wagons went slowly; so I rode on in advance, we arrived at the Isandlwana Camp, went to the Head-Quarters Tent, and got a copy of the orders as affecting me, and found that I was to keep the ponts in working order, and also the road between Helpmakaar and Rorke's Drift and the orders also particularly stated that my duties lay on the right bank of the River Buffalo.

An N.C.O. of the 24th Regiment lent me a field glass, which was a very good one, and I also looked with my own, and could see the enemy moving on the distant hills, and apparently in great force. Large numbers of them moving to my left, until the lion hill of Isandlwana, on my left as I looked at them, hid them from my view. The idea struck me that they might be moving in the direction between the camp and Rorke's Drift and prevent my getting back, and also they might be going to make a dash at the ponts.

Seeing what my duties were, I left the camp, and a quarter of a mile, or less out of it met with Colonel Durnford R.E., riding at the head of his mounted men. I told him what I had seen, and took some orders, and a message all along his line at his request. At the foot of the hill I met my men in the wagon and made them get out and walk up the hill with Durnford's men. I brought the wagon back with me to Rorke's Drift, where on arrival I found the following order had been issued. The copy below was given me, and preserved from the fact of its being in my pocket during the fight:

Camp Rorke's Drift

Camp Morning Orders

22nd January 1879

1. The force under Lt. Col. Durnford R.E., having departed, a Guard of 6 Privates and 1 N.C.O. will be furnished by the detachment 2/24th Regiment on the ponts. A Guard of 50 armed natives will likewise be furnished by Capt. Stevenson's detachment at the same spot. The ponts will be invariably drawn over to the Natal side at night. This

duty will cease on the arrival of Capt. Rainforth's Company 1/24th Regiment.

2. In accordance with para. 19 Regulations for Field Forces in South Africa, Capt. Rainforth's Company, 1/24th Regiment, will entrench itself on the spot assigned to it by Column Orders para.-dated-.

H. Spalding, Major

Commanding

The Guard as detailed was over the ponts. Captain Rainforth's Company had not arrived. I went at once to Major Spalding on arrival, told him what I had seen, and pointed out to him that in the event of an attack on the ponts it would be impossible with 7 men (not counting the natives) to make an effective defence. (According to the orders, Capt. Rainforth's Company should have been already at Rorke's Drift.

Major Spalding told me he was going over to Helpmakaar, and would see about getting it down at once. Just as I was about to ride away he said to me 'Which of you is senior, you or Bromhead?" I said " I don't know" - he went back to his tent, looked at the Army List, and coming back, said "I see you are senior, so you will be in charge, although of course, nothing will happen, and I shall be back again this evening early."

I then went down to my tent by the river, had some lunch comfortably, and was writing a letter home when my attention was called to two horsemen galloping towards us from the direction of Isandlwana. From their gesticulation and their shouts, when they were near enough to be heard, we saw that something was the matter, and on taking them over the river, one of them, Lieutenant Adendorff of Lonsdale's Regiment, Natal Native Contingent, asking if I was an officer, jumped off his horse, took me on one side, and told me that the camp was in the hands of the Zulus and the army destroyed; that scarcely a man had got away to tell the tale, and that probably Lord Chelmsford and the rest of the column had shared the same fate. His companion, a Carbineer, confirmed his story. He was naturally very excited and I am afraid I did not, at first, quite believe him, and intimated that he probably had not remained to see what did occur. I had the saddle put on my horse, and while I was talking to Lieutenant Adendorff, a messenger arrived from Lieutenant Bromhead, who was with his company at his little camp near the commissariat stores, to ask me to come up at once.

I gave the order to inspan the wagon and put all the stores, tents, etc., they could into it. I posted the seargeant and six men on the high ground over the Pont, behind a natural wall of rocks, forming a strong position from which there was a good view over the river and ground in front, with orders to wait until I came or sent for them. The guard of natives had left some time before and had not been relieved. I galloped up at once to the commissariat stores and found that a pencil note had been sent from the 3rd Column by Captain Allan Gardner to state that the enemy were advancing in force against our post. Lieutenant Bromhead had, with the assistance of Mr. Dalton, Dr. Reynolds and the other officers present, commenced barricading and loopholing the store building and the missionary's house, which was used as a hospital, and connecting the defence of the two buildings by walls of mealie bags, and two wagons that were on the ground. The Native Contingent, under their officer, Captain Stephenson, were working hard at this with our own men, and the walls were rapidly progressing. A letter describing what had happened had been sent by Bromhead by two men of the Mounted Infantry, who had arrived fugitives from Isandlwana, to the officer commanding at Helpmakaar. These two men crossed the river at Fugitives Drift, with some others, and as they have since reported to me, came to give notice of what had happened, to us at Rorke's Drift, of their own accord and without orders from anyone.

I held a consultation with Lieutenant Bromhead, and with Mr. Dalton, whose energy, intelligence and gallantry were of the greatest service to us, and whom, as I said in my report at the time, and I am sure Bromhead would unite with me in saying again now, I cannot sufficiently thank for his services. I went round the position with them and then rode down to the ponts where I found everything ready for a start, ponts in midstream, hawsers and cables sunk, etc. It was at this time that the Pontman Daniells, and Sergeant Milne, 3rd Buffs, who had been employed for some time in getting the ponts in order, and working them under Lieutenant MacDowell, R.E., (Killed at Isandlwana), offered to defend the ponts, moored in the middle of the river, from their decks with a few men. Sergeant Williams 24th and his little guard were quite ready to join them.

We arrived at the commissariat store about 3.30 p.m. Shortly afterwards an officer of Durnford's Horse reported his arrival from Isandlwana, and I requested him to observe the movements, and check the advance, of the enemy as much as possible until forced to fall back. I saw each man at his post, and then the work went on again.

Several fugitives from the camp arrived, and tried to impress upon us the madness of an attempt to defend the place. Who they were I do not know, but it is scarcely necessary for me to say that there were no officers of HM Army among them. They stopped the work very much, it being impossible to prevent the men getting around them in little groups to hear their story. They proved the truth of their belief in what they said by leaving us to our fate, and in the state of mind they were in, I think our little garrison was as well without them. As far as I know, but one of the fugitives remained with us - Lieutenant Adendorff, whom I have before mentioned. He remained to assist in the defence, and from a loophole in the store building, flanking the wall and hospital, his rifle did good service.

There were several casks of rum in the store building and I gave strict orders to Sergeant Windridge, 24th Regiment, who was in charge (acting as issuer of commissariat stores to the troops), that the spirit was not to be touched, the man posted nearest it was to be considered on guard over it, and after giving fair warning was to shoot without altercation anyone who attempted to force his post, and Sergeant Windridge being there was to see this carried out. Sergeant Windridge showed great intelligence and energy in arranging the stores of the defence of the commissariat store, forming loopholes etc.

The Reverend George Smith, vicar of Estcourt, Natal, and acting Army chaplain, went for a walk (before the news of the disaster reached us) to the top of the Oscarberg, the hill behind Rorke's Drift. Mr. Witt, the missionary, went with him, or met him there. They went to see what could be seen in the direction of the Isandlwana camp. He saw the force of the enemy which attacked us at Rorke's Drift, cross the river in three bodies, and after snuff taking, and other ceremonies, advance in our direction. He had been watching them for a long time with interest, and thought they were our own Native Contingent. There were two mounted men leading them, and he did not realise they were the enemy until they were near enough for him to see that these two men also had black faces. He came running down the hill and was agreeably surprised to find that we were getting ready for the enemy. Mr. Witt, whose wife and family were in a lonely house not very far off, rode off, taking with him a sick officer, who was very ill in hospital and only just able to ride. Mr. Smith however, although he might well have left, elected to remain with us, and during the attack did good service in supplying the men with ammunition.

About 4.20 p.m. the sound of firing was heard behind the Oscarberg. The officer of Durnford's returned, reporting the enemy close upon us, and that his men would not obey his orders but were going off to

Helpmakaar, and I saw them, about 100 in number, going off in that direction. I have seen these same men behave so well since that I have spoken with several of their conduct - and they all said, as their excuse, that Durnford was killed, and that it was no use. About the same time Captain Stephenson's detachment of Natal Native Contingent left us - probably most fortunately for us. I am sorry to say that their officer, who had been doing good service in getting his men to work, also deserted us. We seemed very few now all these people had gone, and I saw that our line of defence was too extended, and at once commenced a retrenchment of biscuit boxes, so as to get a place we could fall back upon if we could not hold the whole.

Private Hitch, 24th, was on top of the thatch roof of the commissariat store keeping a look-out. He was severely wounded early in the evening, but notwithstanding, with Corporal Allen, 24th, who was also wounded, continued to do good service, and they both when incapacitated by their wounds from using their rifles, still continued under fire serving their comrades with ammunition. We had not completed a wall two boxes high when, about 4.30 p.m., Hitch cried out that the enemy was in sight, and he saw them, apparently 500 or 600 in number, came around the hill to our south (the Oscarberg) and advance at a run against our south wall.

We opened fire on them, between five and six hundred yards, at first a little wild, but only for a short time, a chief on horseback was dropped by Private Dunbar, 24th. The men were quite steady, and the Zulus began to fall very thick. However, it did not seem to stop them at all, although they took advantage of the cover and ran stooping with their faces near the ground. It seemed as if nothing would stop them, and they rushed on in spite of their heavy loss to within 50 yards of the wall, when they were taken in flank by the fire from the end wall of the store building, and met with such a heavy direct fire from the mealie wall, and the hospital at the same time, that they were checked as if by magic.

They occupied the cook house ovens, banks and other cover, but the greater number, without stopping, moved to their left around the hospital, and made a rush at the end of the hospital, and at our north-west line of mealie bags. There was a short but desperate struggle during which Mr. Dalton shot a Zulu who was in the act of assegaing a corporal of the Army Hospital Corps, the muzzle of whose rifle he had seized, and with Lieutenant Bromhead and many of the men behaved with great gallantry. The Zulus forced us back from that part of the wall immediately in front of the hospital, but after suffering very severely in the struggle were driven back into the bush around our position.

The main body of the enemy were close behind the first force which appeared, and had lined the ledge of rocks and caves in the Oscarberg overlooking us, and about three or four hundred yards to our south, from where they kept up a constant fire. Advancing somewhat more to their left than the first attack, they occupied the garden, hollow road, and bush in great force. The bush grew close to our wall and we had not had time to cut it down. The enemy were thus able to advance under cover close to our wall, and in this part soon held one side of the wall, while we held the other.

A series of desperate assaults were made, on the hospital, and extending from the hospital, as far as the bush reached; but each was most splendidly met and repulsed by our men, with the bayonet. Each time as the attack was repulsed by us, the Zulus close to us seemed to vanish in the bush, those some little distance off keeping up a fire all the time. Then, as if moved by a single impulse, they rose up in the bush as thick as possible rushing madly up to the wall (some of them being already close to it), seizing, where they could, the muzzles of our men's rifles, or their bayonets, and attempting to use their assegais and to get over the wall. A rapid rattle of fire from our rifles, stabs with the bayonet, and in a few moments the Zulus were driven back, disappearing in the bush as before, and keeping up their fire. A brief interval and the attack would be again made, and repulsed in the same manner. Over and over again this happened, our men behaving with the greatest coolness and gallantry. It is impossible for one individual to see all, but I particularly myself noticed the behaviour of Colour Sergeant Bourne 24tth, Private McMahon, AHC, Privates Roy, Deacon, Bush, Cole, Jenkins 24th, and many others.

Our fire at the time of these rushes of the Zulus was very rapid. Mr. Dalton dropping a man each time he fired his rifle, while Bromhead and myself used our revolvers. The fire from the rocks and caves on the hill behind us was kept up all this time and took us completely in reverse, and although very badly directed, many shots came among us and caused us some loss, and at about 6.00 p.m. the enemy extending their attack further to their left, I feared seriously would get it over our wall behind the biscuit boxes. I ran back with two or three men to this part of the wall and was immediately joined by Bromhead with two or three more. The enemy stuck to this assault most tenaciously, and on their repulse, and retiring into the bush, I called all the men inside our retrenchment and the enemy immediately occupied the wall we had abandoned and used it as a breastwork to fire over.

Mr. Byrne, acting Commissariat Officer, and who had behaved with great coolness and gallantry, was killed instantaneously shortly before this by a bullet through the head, just after he had given a drink of water to a wounded man of the NNC.

All this time the enemy had been attempting to fire the hospital and had at length set fire to its roof and got in at the far end. I had tried to impress upon the men in the hospital the necessity for making a communication right through the building – unfortunately this was not done. Probably at the time the men could not see the necessity, and doubtless also there was no time to do it. Without in the least detracting from the gallant fellows who defended the hospital, and I hope I shall not be misunderstood in saying so, I have always regretted, as I did then, the absence of my four poor sappers, who had only left that morning for Isandlwana and arrived there just to be killed.

The garrison of the hospital defended it with the greatest gallantry, room by room, bringing out all the sick that could be moved, and breaking through some of the partitions while the Zulus were in the building with them. Private Williams, Hook, R. Jones and W.Jones being the last to leave and holding the doorway with the bayonet, their ammunition being expended. Private Williams's bayonet was wrenched off his rifle by a Zulu, but with the other men he still managed with the muzzle of his rifle to keep the enemy at bay. Surgeon Reynolds carried his arms full of ammunition to the hospital, a bullet striking his helmet as he did so. But we were too busily engaged outside to be able to do much, and with the hospital on fire, and no free communication, nothing could have saved it. Sergeant Maxfield 24th might have been saved, but he was delirious with fever, refused to move and resisted the attempts to move him. He was assegaid before our men's eyes.

Seeing the hospital burning, and the attempts of the enemy to fire the roof of the store (one man was shot, I believe by Lt. Adendorff who had a light almost touching the thatch), we converted two large heaps of mealie bags into a sort of redoubt which gave a second line of fire all around, in case the store building had to be abandoned, or the enemy broke through elsewhere. Assistant Commissary Dunne worked hard at this, and from his height, being a tall man, he was much exposed, in addition to the fact that the heaps were high above our walls, and that most of the Zulu bullets went high.

Trooper Hunter, Natal Mounted Police, escaping from the hospital, stood still for a moment, hesitating which way to go, dazed by the glare of the burning hospital, and the firing that was going on all around. He was assegaid before our eyes, the Zulu who killed him immediately afterwards falling. While firing from behind the biscuit boxes, Dalton, who had been using his rifle with deadly effect, and by his quickness and coolness had been the means of saving many men's lives, was shot through the body. I was standing near him at the time, and he handed me his rifle so coolly that I had no idea until afterwards of how severely he was wounded. He waited quite quietly for me to take the cartridges he had left out of his pockets. We put him inside our mealie sack redoubt, building it up around him. About this time I noticed Private Dunbar 24th make some splendid shooting, seven or eight Zulus falling on the ledge of rocks in the Oscarberg to as many consecutive shots by him. I saw Corporal Lyons hit by a bullet which lodged in his spine, and fall between an opening we had left in the wall of biscuit boxes. I thought he was killed, but looking up he said, "Oh, Sir! You are not going to leave me here like a dog?" We pulled him in and laid him down behind the boxes where he was immediately looked to by Reynolds. Corporal Scamle (Scammell) of the Natal Native Contingent, who was badly wounded through the shoulder, staggered out under fire again, from the store building where he had been put, and gave me all his cartridges, which in his wounded state he could not use. While I was intently watching to get a fair shot at a Zulu who appeared to be firing rather well, Private Jenkins 24th, saying "Look out, Sir," gave my head a duck down just as a bullet whizzed over it. He had noticed a Zulu who was quite near in another direction taking a deliberate aim at me. For all the man could have known, the shot might have been directed at himself. I mention these facts to show how well the men behaved and how loyally worked together.

Corporal Schiess, Natal Native Contingent, who was a patient in the hospital with a wound in the foot, which caused him great pain, behaved with the greatest coolness and gallantry throughout the attack, and at this time creeping out a short distance along the wall we had abandoned, and slowly raising himself, to get a shot at some of the enemy who had been particularly annoying, his hat was blown off by a shot from a zulu the other side of the wall. He immediately jumped up, bayoneted the Zulu and shot a second, and bayoneted a third who came to their assistance, and then returned to his place.

As darkness came on we were completely surrounded. The Zulus wrecking the camp of the Company 24th and my wagon which had been left outside, in spite of the efforts of my batman, Driver Robson (the only man of the Royal Engineers with us), who had directed his particular attention to keeping the Zulus off this wagon in which we were, as he described it, "Our things".

They also attacked the east end of our position, and after being several times repulsed, eventually got into the kraal, which was strongly built with high walls, and drove us to the middle, and then to the inner wall of the kraal - the enemy occupying the middle wall as we abandoned it. This wall was too high for them to use it effectively to fire over, and a Zulu no sooner showed his head over it than he was dropped, being so close that it was almost impossible to miss him. Shortly before this, some of the men said they saw the red-coats coming on the Helpmakaar road. The rumour passed quickly round. I could see nothing of the sort myself, but some men said they could. A cheer was raised, and the enemy seemed to pause, to know what it meant, but there was no answer to it, and darkness came. It is very strange that this report should have arisen amongst us, for the two companies 24th from Helpmakaar did come to the foot of the hill, but not, I believe, in sight of us. They marched back to Helpmakaar on the report of Rorke's Drift having fallen.

After the first onslaught, the most formidable of the enemy's attacks was just before we retired behind our line of biscuit boxes, and for a short time after it, when they had gained great confidence by their success on the hospital. Although they kept their positions behind the walls we had abandoned, and kept up a heavy fire from all sides until about 12 0'clock, they did not actually charge up in a body to get over our wall after about 9 or 10 o'clock. After this time it became very dark, although the hospital roof was still burning - it was impossible from below to see what was going on, and Bromhead and myself getting up on the mealy sack redoubt, kept an anxious watch on all sides.

The enemy were now in strong force all around us, and every now and then a confused shout of "Usutu" from many voices seemed to show that they were going to attack from one side and immediately the same thing would happen on the other, leaving us in doubt as to where they meant to attack. About midnight or a little after the fire slackened and after that, although they kept us constantly on the alert, by feigning, as before, to come on at different points, the fire was of a desultory character. Our men were careful, and only fired when they could see a fair chance. The flame of the burning hospital was now getting low, and as pieces of the roof fell, or hitherto unburnt parts of the thatch ignited, the flames would blaze up illuminating our helmets and faces. A few shots from the Zulus, replied to by our men - again silence, broken only by the same thing repeatedly happening. This sort of thing went on until about 4 a.m. and we were anxiously waiting for daybreak and the renewal of the attack, which their comparative, and at length complete silence, led us to expect. But at daybreak the enemy were out of sight, over the hill to our south west. One Zulu had remained in the kraal and fired a shot among us (without doing any damage) as we stood on the walls, and ran off in the direction of the river - although many shots were fired at him as he ran. I am glad to say the plucky fellow got off.

Taking care not to be surprised by any ruse of the enemy, we patrolled the ground around the place, collecting the arms, and ammunition, of the dead Zulus.

Some of the bullet wounds were very curious. One man's head was split open, exactly as if done with an axe. Another had been hit just between the eyes, the bullet carrying away the whole of the back of his head, leaving his face perfect, as though it were a mask, only disfigured by the small hole made by the bullet passing through. One of the wretches we found, one hand grasping a bench that had been dragged from the hospital, and sustained thus in the position we found him in, while in the other hand he still clutched the knife with which he had mutilated one of our poor fellows, over whom he was still leaning.

We increased the strength of our defences as much as possible, strengthening and raising our walls, putting sacks on the biscuit boxes, etc., and were removing the thatch from the roof of the commissariat store, to avoid being burnt out in case of another attack, when at about 7 a.m. a large body of the enemy (I believe the same who had attacked us) appeared on the hills to the south west. I thought at the time that they were going to attack us, but from what I now know from the Zulus, and also of the number we put hors de combat, I do not think so. I think that they came up on the high ground to observe Lord Chelmsford's advance; from there they could see the column long before it came in sight of us.

A frightened and fugitive (auxiliary) came in shortly before and I sent for Daniells the pontman, who could speak Zulu a little, to interview him. Daniells had armed himself with Spalding's sword, which he flourished in so wild and eccentric a manner that the poor wretch thought his last hour had come. He professed to be friendly and to have escaped from Isandlwana, and I sent him with a note to the officer commanding at Helpmakaar, explaining our situation, and asking for help: for now, although the men were in excellent spirits, and each man had a good supply of ammunition in his pouches, we had only about a box and a half left besides, and at this time we had no definite knowledge of what had happened, and I myself did not know that the part of the Column with Lord Chelmsford had taken any part in the action at Isandlwana, or whether on the camp being taken he had fallen back on Helpmakaar.

The enemy remained on the hill, and still more of them appeared, when about 8 a.m. the column came in sight, and the enemy disappeared again. There were a great many of our Native Levies with the column, and the number of redcoats seemed so few that at first we had grave doubts that the force approaching was the enemy. We improvised a flag, and our signals were soon replied to from the column. The mounted men crossed the drift and galloped up to us, headed by Major Cecil Russell and Lieutenant Walsh, and were received by us with a hearty cheer. Lord Chelmsford, with his staff, shortly after rode up and thanked us all with much emotion for the defence we had made. The column arrived, crossing by the ponts, and we then had a busy time in making a strong position for the night.

I was glad to seize an opportunity to wash my face in a muddy puddle, in company with Private Bush 24th, whose face was covered with blood from a wound in the nose caused by the bullet which had passed through and killed Private Cole 24th. With the politeness of a soldier, he lent me his towel, or, rather, a very dirty half of one, before using it himself, and I was very glad to accept it.

In wrecking the stores in my wagon, the Zulus had brought to light a forgotten bottle of beer, and Bromhead and I drank it with mutual congratulations on having come safely out of so much danger.

My wagon driver, a Cape (coloured) man, lost his courage on hearing the first firing around the hill. He let loose his mules and retreated, concealing himself in one of the caves of the Oscarberg. He saw the Zulus run by him and, to his horror, some of them entered the cave he was in, and lying down commenced firing at us. The poor wretch was crouching in the darkness, in the far depths of the cave, afraid to speak or move, and our bullets came into the cave killing one of the Zulus. He did not know from whom he was in the most danger, friends or foes, and came down in the morning looking more dead than alive. The mules we recovered; they were quietly grazing by the riverside.

On my journey homewards, on arriving at the railway station, Durban, I asked a porter to get me some Kaffirs to carry my bags to the hotel. He sent several, and the first to come running up was my voorlooper boy who had taken me up to Rorke's Drift. He stopped short and looked very frightened, and I believe at first though he saw my ghost. I seized him to prevent his running away, and when he saw that I was flesh and blood he became reassured. He said he thought I had been killed, and upon my asking him how he thought I got away, he said (the solution of the mystery just striking him), "I know you rode away on the other horse." As far as I could learn and according to his own story, the boy had taken the horse I rode up from the river to the commissariat store, and wild with terror, had ridden it to Pietermaritzburg without stopping, where he gave it to the Transport people, but having no certificate to say who he was, they took the horse from him but would not give him any employment.

During the fight there were some very narrow escapes from the burning hospital. Private Waters, 24th Regiment, told me that he had secreted himself in a cupboard in the room he was defending, and from it shot several Zulus inside the hospital. He was wounded in the arm, and he remained in the cupboard until the heat and smoke were so great that they threatened to suffocate him. Wrapping himself in a cloak, or skirt of a dress he found in the cupboard, he rushed out into the darkness and made his way into the cookhouse. The Zulus were occupying this, and firing at us from the wall nearest us. It was too late to retreat, so he crept softly to the fireplace and, standing up in the chimney, blacked his face and hands with the soot. He remained there until the Zulus left. He was very nearly shot in coming out, one of our men at the wall raising his rifle to do so at the sight of his black face and strange costume, but Waters cried out just in time to save himself. He produced the bullet that wounded him, with pardonable pride, and was very amusing in his admiring description of Dr. Reynold's skill in extracting it.

Gunner Howard, R.A., ran out of the burning hospital, through the enemy, and lay down on the upper side of the wall in front of our N parapet. The bodies of several horses that were killed early in the evening were lying here, and concealed by these and by Zulu bodies and the low grass and bushes, he remained unseen with the Zulus all around him until they left in the morning.

Private Becket, 24th Regiment, escaped from the hospital in the same direction, he was badly wounded with assegais in running through the enemy. He managed to get away and conceal himself in the ditch of the garden, where we found him the next morning. The poor fellow was so weak from loss of blood that he could not walk, and he died shortly afterwards.

Our mealie - bag walls were afterwards replaced by loopholed walls of stone, the work making rapid progress upon the arrival of half the 5th Company R.E. with Lieutenant Porter. As soon as the Sappers arrived we put a fence around, and a rough wood cross over, the graves of our poor men who were killed. This was afterwards replaced by a neat stone monument and inscription by the 24th, who remained to garrison the place.

I have already in my report, said how gallantly all behaved, from

Lieutenant Bromhead downwards, and I also mentioned those whom I had particularly noticed to have distinguished themselves.

On the day following, we buried 351 bodies of the enemy in graves not far from the Comissarriat Buildings - many bodies were since discovered and buried, and when I was sick at Ladysmith one of our Sergeants, who came down there invalided from Rorke's Drift, where he had been employed in the construction of Fort Melvill, told me that many Zulu bodies were found in the caves and among the rocks, a long distance from the Mission house, when getting stone for that fort. As in my report, I underestimated the number we killed, so I believe I also underestimated the number of the enemy that attacked us, and from what I have since learned I believe the Zulus must have numbered at least 4,000.

As the Reverend George Smith said in a short account he wrote to a Natal paper - "Whatever signs of approval may be conferred upon the defenders of Rorke's Drift, from the high quarters, they will never cease to remember the kind and heartfelt expressions of gratitude which have fallen both from the columns of the Colonial Press and from so many of the Natal Colonists themselves."

And to this may I add that they will ever remember with heartfelt gratitude the signs of approval that have been conferred upon them by their Sovereign and by the People and the Press of England.

John R.M. Chard,
Captain and Bt. Major, R.E.
January 1880

POPULARLY BELIEVED MYTHS ABOUT RORKE'S DRIFT (HISTORICAL FACT VERSUS CINEMATOGRAPHICAL FICTION)

- The battle of Rorke's Drift took place mostly at night. Beginning at 1630hrs on the 22 January 1879 and ending twelve hours later shortly after dawn on the 23 January 1879.

- The British Army Unit involved was B Company of the 24th Regiment of Foot (2nd Warwickshires) a regiment that did not change its title to the South Wales Borders until 1 July 1881, two and a half years after the battle. The proportion of Welshmen in the regiment did not exceed 20% and was likely to be less than that. The 24th Regiment of Foot consisted of men from England, Ireland, Wales and Scotland.

- The 'real' hero of Rorke's Drift was an Irishman, Acting Assistant Commissary James Langley Dalton. It was largely his experience that proved vital to the defence of Rorke's Drift.

- The Zulus used mostly obsolete rifles in poor repair at Rorke's Drift and not the British Martini-Henry rifles taken from the field after their earlier success at the Battle of Isandlwana. It was the

145

Zulu reserve, largely uninvolved at that battle, that moved onto Rorke's Drift.

- There was no 'Salute to the Brave' rendered by the Zulus to the victorious defenders of Rorke's Drift at the battle's end. The arrival of the relief column, arriving when it did, put an end to any continuance of hostilities, the Zulus retreating .

- The Zulu wounded lying around the post were shot or bayoneted for the most part by the relief column who had come from Isandlwana and had seen for themselves the state of the British dead there.

BIBLIOGRAPHY

Gillings, Ken, *Discovering the Battlefields of the Anglo-Zulu War*, 30 Degrees South Publishers, South Africa 2014

Glover, Michael, *Rorke's Drift*, Wordsworth, Hertfordshire 1997.

Knight, Ian, McBride Angus, *The Zulus*, Osprey London 1991.

Knight, Ian, Perry Michael & Alan, *Rorke's Drift 1879*, Osprey, London 1996.

Knight, Ian, *Great Zulu Battles 1838-1906*, Castle Books, London 1998.

Knight, Ian, *Zulu Rising – The Epic Story of Isandlwana and Rorke's Drift,* Macmillan, Oxford 2010.

Ritter, F.A., *Shaka Zulu,* Longmans, Green and Co. Ltd., London 1960.

Snook, Mike, Lieutenant-Colonel, *How Can Man Die Better? – The Secrets of Isandlwana Revealed,* Frontline Books, London 2005.

Snook, Mike, Lieutenant-Colonel, *Like wolves on the fold - The Defence of Rorke's Drift,* Greenhill Books, London 2006.

ACKNOWLEDGEMENTS

When I was 12, my English homework required one evening a short written description of a battle. I set about the task with an energised eagerness and committed gusto, giving a lively, stirring and vivid account with enthusiastically detailed depiction and fulsome flowing narrative, including the use of the term 'fierce fighting'. Some of the descriptions were then read aloud by the teacher, mine amongst them, and the effort deemed worthy, but my use of the phrase 'fierce fighting' came in for mention as being superfluous. After all, was not the adjective already implied in the verb, was not all fighting fierce? The teacher was the teacher and I accepted the point, but even at 12 years of age I knew – because these are matters 12-year-old boys know – when it comes to fighting there are different degrees, duration and dynamics involved. That was then, this is now, and after almost forty years of being a soldier I know there are many variants of violence, categories of conflict, and classifications of combat and fighting can take many forms from faint-hearted to, yes, fierce.

In this book I am a soldier telling a soldiers story. It is a particular perspective. The Anglo-Zulu War of 1879 at the strategic level was an unwanted war, at the operational level, an unnecessary war, at the tactical level, a war that had nonetheless to be fought and won by soldiers. It is the politician that commits a nation to war, it is the soldier who has to sort out the mess. The engagement against Zulu assault at Rorke's Drift involved a defence so vigorous, a contest so immediate, that there was only the now of the hand-to-hand combat that counted, the moment that mattered, lose that moment, and everything was lost. The fighting was as ferocious as it was fiery, as frenetic as it was, yes, fierce!

For its telling I wish to very gratefully acknowledge the uncompromising rigor of Barry Bradfield's research, for his unerring capacity to unearth a wealth of valuable detail, an expertise that has singularly contributed enormously to the text and so to the truth of the matter. To Maurice Sweeney whose unstinting editorial 'over watch' ensured the intended story was told without a superfluity yet with a necessary vitality to the narrative that the subject demanded. I would like to also thank Ray Kirpatrick, military illustrator, whose work for this book, including its front cover, exemplifies the notion that 'memory is well served by imagery'. The input of Richard Davis, curator of the Regimental Museum of the Royal Welsh in Brecon Wales, was indeed very valuable. My gratitude also goes to Fintan O'Connell, Inspire Printers, Skibbereen, Co. Cork, and his excellent staff for the degree of interest and excellence they displayed in getting right the book's physical production, giving full meaning to the saying, 'People want what's beautiful'. Finally, but very fervently to Ken Gillings, South African military historian and battlefield guide whose knowledge is matched only by his enthusiasm for his subject; time spent in his company proved a positive joy, days passing like hours, such was his interest in imparting an awareness and understanding of all that was relevant towards achieving a commanding comprehension of the detail of the battle. A special thank you to Eva, Lynn, Mary-Claire, and Hugo whose encouragement empowered my efforts. It is for their generation I write: that they will know, what ours did not, about the Irish at Rorke's Drift.

INDEX

C

D

E

F

G

R

S

T

U

V